BROWSE

The World in Bookshops

EDITED BY

Henry Hitchings

PUSHKIN PRESS

Pushkin Press
71–75 Shelton Street, London WC2H 9JQ

Browse: The World In Bookshops first published in 2016

Copyright in the arrangement © Pushkin Press 2016

Introduction © Henry Hitchings 2016

'If You Wound a Snake…' © Alaa Al Aswany 2016; 'La Palmaverde' © Stefano
Benni 2016; 'Snow Day' © Michael Dirda 2016; 'Dussmann: A Conversation' ©
Daniel Kehlmann 2016; 'Something That Doesn't Exist' © Andrey Kurkov 2016;
'All that Offers a Happy Ending Is a Fairy Tale' © Yiyun Li 2016; 'A Bookshop
in the Age of Progress' © Pankaj Mishra 2016; 'Intimacy' © Dorthe Nors 2016;
'Desiderium: The Accidental Bookshop of Nairobi' © Yvonne Adhiambo
Owuor; 'The Pillars of Hercules' © Ian Sansom 2016; 'My Homeland Is
Storyland' © Elif Shafak 2016; 'Bohemia Road' © Iain Sinclair 2016; 'Bookshop
Time' © Ali Smith 2016; 'Leitner and I' © Saša Stanišić 2016; 'A Tale of Two
Bookshops' © Juan Gabriel Vásquez 2016

ISBN 978 1 782272 12 0

10 9 8 7 6 5 4 3 2

Set in Monotype Sabon by Tetragon, London
Printed and bound by CPI Group (UK) Ltd, Croydon CR0 4YY

www.pushkinpress.com

CONTENTS

Introduction:
A Place to Pause

HENRY HITCHINGS

I 'm nine years old, and I've been given a book token for my birthday. My mother takes me to spend it. The shop, all polished wood and green carpet, makes me think of a billiard table. I've recently read and enjoyed Frank Herbert's *Dune*, a novel full of characters with names that strike even a nine-year-old as quaintly improbable (Duncan Idaho, Wellington Yueh), so I pick out the sequel, *Dune Messiah*, and then I grab the next two volumes in the series, *Children of Dune* and *God Emperor Dune*. "Who are you trying to impress?" asks another shopper, before adding, "The best one's *Beach Party on Dune*." "I haven't heard of it," I say sheepishly, and he laughs.

Recalling this now, I can picture exactly what the *Dune* books looked like, even though I gave up on the series halfway through the second volume. But it's the book that didn't exist that looms largest in my imagination; *Beach Party on Dune* really ought to have been written—hello again, Duncan Idaho—and sometimes I fantasize about finding a bookshop so profusely stocked that it'll be there.

In 1939 Jorge Luis Borges published an essay in which he pictured a "total library" containing every possible book, and he returned to this theme in his story "La biblioteca de Babel", visualizing a library that encompassed "all that is able to be expressed, in every language". What I have in mind is a variant on this: a total bookshop, which includes, like Borges's library, a faithful catalogue of all it contains, a panoply of false catalogues, proofs of the falsity of the false catalogues, proof of the falsity of the true catalogue…

I'm fifteen, and at the local bookshop, a single bright room with tall white shelves, there's a large display stand dominated by Picador and Faber paperbacks, all of which look enticing. For a couple of weeks I eye up *The Great Shark Hunt*—a chunky collection of Hunter S. Thompson's journalism, dense with trippy verbiage. (Looking back, I'm not sure why I didn't buy it, but wonder if perhaps it was beyond my schoolboy budget.) One day, while flicking through *The Great Shark Hunt*, I'm distracted by a friend who wants to go and procure some Nerds—sweets that are like fizzy drips of candle wax—and it's only when I am a hundred yards from the shop that I realize I have liberated the book. I now face the challenge of returning it, undetected. It would be easier to keep it, of course, and part of me is willing to pretend that Hunter S. Thompson is the sort of writer whose books one ought to steal. But instead I go back and try to sneak *The Great Shark Hunt* into its rightful place on the display stand—except the stand chooses this moment to revolve extravagantly, and I almost knock it over, and then it almost knocks me over, and the shop's proprietor, who resembles an angry hawk, swoops in to ask me what the hell I'm doing.

Throughout my teens, bookshops served as places of furtive self-education. I still like the idea that a bookshop can be an informal library, though not a lending library, and I know I learnt a lot about literature by snooping around well-stocked fiction sections. I can remember catching a production of *Who's Afraid of Virginia Woolf?* at a time when I knew nothing of Virginia Woolf; I concluded that she was someone I ought to be daunted by, and it was therefore a thrill, not long afterwards, to see a whole shelf of her novels (the Oxford World's Classics editions, each with a yellow spine and a flash of red at the top) and to pluck down *Orlando* and start reading.

"He—for there could be no doubt of his sex, though the fashion of the time did something to disguise it…" What madness was this? The very words "There could be no doubt of his sex" created room for doubt, and I was hooked. The next paragraph, nearly three pages long, contained a word I'd never seen before, *asphodel*, and the febrile pleasure of encounter caused me to collide with another customer, who clearly—and not unreasonably, though incorrectly—thought this was my idea of flirtation. So much to know. So much to find out. And always the sense of the bookshop itself as a cabinet of curiosities, a time machine, and a place of minor embarrassments.

I'm eighteen, and I am holding a copy of Ezra Pound's *Cantos*. This is in Blackwell's bookshop in Oxford, in the second-hand department, a place where earnestness goes to ramify and breed—and where all the stock seems overpriced but also either urgently necessary or naggingly desirable. Pound's *Cantos* is a mixture of the two: I ought to be familiar with these poems, given that I'm about to study modernism, and this particular copy, with Henri Gaudier-Brzeska's sketch of Pound on the spine, is in mint condition. I turn it over several times, trying to work out how it'll fit in with the bedlam of my student bookshelves. A voice intrudes: "You won't understand that." It emanates from the beard of a visiting scholar I've previously noticed haunting the English faculty library, and he removes the book from my hand and says to his young companion, "If I press this on you, will you read it?" I want to tell him that the volume is mine and that he's a shit-breeched poltroon who shouldn't be pressing anything on anyone. But he beats me to the punch: "Stick to the easy stuff, little man."

At eighteen, the easy stuff was the last thing I wanted. I was determined to stretch myself, to augment my reality. Pound's sprawling, refractory epic, with its fusion of personal and intellectual history, was precisely what I was after.

I recently reread the *Cantos*, inspired to do so by visiting San Michele, the island in the Venetian lagoon where

Pound is buried—and where, in the driving June rain, I was wretchedly incapable of locating his grave. Now I look again at my copy of the book. I've written the date inside: 2nd November 1993. *Hmmm.* I was eighteen then, so maybe the visiting scholar's young companion wasn't persuaded after all.

I'm twenty-six, and I'm in the City Lights Bookstore in San Francisco, which is famous for having been founded by the poet Lawrence Ferlinghetti (and less famous for having been co-founded by Peter D. Martin, who was the son of the anti-fascism crusader Carlo Tresca). I have read Ferlinghetti and think of him as an indescribably romantic figure—the name helps, and so does the fact that he published Allen Ginsberg's *Howl* and was prosecuted on account of its alleged obscenity. For half an hour I nose around the shop, which somehow puts me in mind of an abandoned tram; I manage to avoid being the rube who asks "Where's Ferlinghetti today?", and I buy a copy of *McSweeney's*, a newish and much-admired literary magazine I have heard of yet never previously seen. It's a hardback, costing about double what I paid for my dinner. But it contains a 44-track CD, each piece of music on it corresponding to an item in the magazine; so, for instance, there's a one-page short story by Lydia Davis, "Oral History with Hiccups", and the track that goes with it, by They Might Be Giants, is called "Drinkin'" and is an instrumental number featuring a bass saxophone, presumably played by John Linnell, who came ninth in *People* magazine's poll of The Most Beautiful People of 1998. The guy manning the cash register looks like he knows all of this. He spins the hardback on the counter, grins, and says, "So now you're part of the problem."

The problem? When I replay this episode in my mind, I think he was joking. I entertain the possibility that he regarded me as yet another chin-stroking try-hard, but conclude that he saw me for what I was: a little too eager to be tasting the cool new flavours, but worth encouraging. He wanted me to feel like I was tapping into something edgy, or at least fresh.

So, the "problem" is a good one. A bookshop can be a magnet for mavericks and nomads. A community hub, a haven, a platform for cultural events. A centre of dissent and radicalism. A place to disseminate notions too strange or explosive for mass circulation. A means of creating and nurturing coteries of readers. These ideas surface repeatedly in this volume: I think of Alaa Al Aswany's image of a bookshop as a mustering point for participants in Egypt's 2011 revolution and of Andrey Kurkov's portrait of Bukinist, a nerve centre for the artistic life of Chernivtsi, Ukraine's so-called Little Vienna.

A final note about City Lights: not long ago I read an interview with some of the shop's current staff, and one, Tân Khánh Cao, reported that "For a while there was a woman who used to sneak in a staff door, and slide down the wooden chute into the room we receive books in. She made herself a bed out of bubble wrap at the bottom of the chute and was found asleep several times." That's not the kind of hospitality generally expected of bookshops, yet it seems apt in the case of City Lights, which has always prided itself on being a cradle of democracy.

I'm twenty-nine, and I am in a bookshop on Charing Cross Road in London. One of those time-warped bunkers that's all dark wood and bile. I've gone in because there's an eighteenth-century copy of Samuel Johnson's *Dictionary of the English Language* in the window. I wrote my doctoral thesis on Johnson, and I'd love to own his *Dictionary*. I ask which edition it is. The man guarding the till looks me up and down. "The sixth." I know that the sixth edition was published in 1785, the year after Johnson's death. I ask the price, and he tells me I can't afford it, and I say I wouldn't mind knowing in any case, and he explains that some old books are hard to come by and are as a result valuable, and I say I know, and then he says that my big overcoat makes me look like a shoplifter and I'd better shove off or he'll call the police.

What would the police have done? At the time (2004) it wasn't yet the norm to get arrested for wearing a heavy overcoat. Perhaps my offence was to blunder into one of those bookshops—less common now than they used to be—where the stock isn't really for sale and the establishment's *raison d'être* is to provide employment for people constitutionally unsuited to any form of work requiring social competence.

There is another side to this, I know. In his jaundiced essay "Bookshop Memories", George Orwell recalls the customers who plagued him when he toiled at Booklovers' Corner in Hampstead, which he did while writing his novel *Keep the Aspidistra Flying*. It wasn't "a kind of paradise where charming old gentlemen browse eternally among calf-bound folios", and his presence was welcome not because he knew about literature, but because he was tall and could reach the shop's highest shelves without a ladder. He had to attend to students trying to find cheap copies of textbooks and to "vague-minded women looking for birthday presents for their nephews". "Many of the people who came to us," he writes, "were of the kind who would be a nuisance anywhere but have special opportunities in a bookshop."

No doubt there have been times when I've been one of those people. Sometimes annoyingly pedantic. Sometimes annoyingly inexact: "I've seen this book. I remember it's got a white cover. I think it's about the brain…"

I'm forty-one, and I am in The Bookseller Crow, in Crystal Palace—named after one of its owners, and also apparently in homage to the scavenging birds that terrorize visitors to the nearby park. It's a defiantly independent bookshop; according to my copy of the London Bookshop Map, it's one of 107 in the city, and "has the widest selection of UK and US titles south of the river". I select Tom Drury's novel *The End of Vandalism*. The man behind the counter, whom I later identify as co-owner Jonathan Main, mentions that he was instrumental in getting the book published in the UK, more than twenty years after it came out in the US.

I've been to bookshops that sell coffee and cakes, and I know of one that's a Thai restaurant, and I've chanced upon several that seem to function as drop-in centres for the desperate. There's a common assumption today that, in order to thrive, bookshops need to be good at things other than selling books. Yet what I look for in a bookshop is still a passion for books themselves. Not a front-foot, evangelizing passion, but the kind of ardour that expresses itself as a desire to have stock that other shops don't have and to represent the world of books with sensitivity and conviction. The kind of ardour that may even lead the bookseller to intervene, just occasionally, in the production and reproduction of literature.

I'm thirty-seven and on a walking holiday in Norfolk. One afternoon in Burnham Market I stop for a sandwich and what I allege will be a quick browse at the Brazen Head Bookshop, which occupies several rooms in an old, porridgy-looking house. I'm not quick. I do, however, manage to choke back the urge to buy half a dozen volumes, and emerge with only one—the Victorian diary of Benjamin Armstrong. I have been seduced by an entry in which he records going to a disappointing party: "small rooms, piano out of tune, bad wine, and stupid people."

This is a pretty tart assessment, and seems all the more pointed for its author being a clergyman.

Inspecting my purchase as I leave, I find a train ticket inside: Cambridge to Norwich, first class. What's this? An academic shuttling between seats of learning? Some latter-day Benjamin Armstrong jaunting between cathedral cities? An upwardly mobile footballer hoping for an advantageous transfer? Fanciful, I know. Yet such is a second-hand book's power to enchant.

Virginia Woolf wrote that "Second-hand books are wild books, homeless books; they have come together in vast flocks of variegated feather, and have a charm which the domesticated volumes of the library lack." The vaster the flocks, the more variegated, and, as Michael Dirda comments in his essay here, "in overwhelming abundance lies the possibility of overlooked treasure". But whatever its size, a colony of second-hand books always has an evocative smell. At the risk of sounding like a breathless oenophile, I'd claim that among its usual scents are almond and vanilla, a grassy sweetness, damp wood and even a hint of mushroom; teased by these aromas, I find myself in a forest, able to slip between worlds or between times, hopeful that behind some of the dark leaves there are golden ones.

Every second-hand shop is an opportunity for a treasure hunt, and is crammed with stories, since every item on its shelves comes with extra layers of history—the traces of past owners, their scribbled marginalia and Post-it notes.

Their rail tickets. I once bought a copy of Elizabeth Barrett Browning's *Selected Poems* that contained, as a makeshift bookmark, the wrapper from a condom. *How do I love thee? Let me count the ways.*

In her essay "Bookshop Time", Ali Smith writes of how "We leave ourselves in our books via this seeming detritus". Discarded books are "repositories of the lives they've been so close to", and a second-hand bookshop is a museum of special moments in those lives. Many of these are acknowledged in the form of inscriptions—melancholy items, since they were fondly written and received by people who are probably now dead.

One of the strangest inscriptions in any second-hand book I've bought is in my copy of Antal Szerb's *Journey by Moonlight*; it's essentially a declaration of love, framed in an oblique style that some might consider quintessentially English, and it is therefore more than a little sad that I acquired the book in a charity shop just a few weeks after the date that appears at the foot of the page.

I'm thirty-one, and I'm in Buenos Aires. My friend Ben, who is not a big reader, insists we visit El Ateneo (or, to give it its full name, El Ateneo Grand Splendid), a bookshop that occupies what was once a theatre and preserves its elaborate frescoes and carvings. At first it appears ordinary, but then I'm in a brightly lit auditorium, straining to look up at the balconies and painted ceiling. I decide I must buy something by Borges; I've read his stories in translation, and now, although my Spanish is nowhere near good enough for me to attempt them in the original, I feel obliged to kid myself that I'm equipped to do so and that maybe I can improve my command of the language by swimming in the Argentine master's prose. Not that his prose is a place to immerse oneself, exactly, since it's so abrupt and epigrammatic—frugal, even. But I've yet to become aware of this. As I examine a paperback of Borges's *Ficciones*, another browsing shopper tells me I must read Adolfo Bioy Casares; when my fumbling reply makes it clear that I'm uncomfortable speaking Spanish, he switches to English and tells me that Casares is "more clever even than Borges". An older man chips in to say that Casares was married to Silvina Ocampo, whose stories are "like dreams", and then his companion wants to know if I have read Julio Cortázar. I haven't, and she steers me to where Cortázar's novels are kept. "The best is *Rayuela*," she tells me, "but it is difficult." I ask if she could recommend something more accessible, and she laughs. "Nothing of Cortázar is easy. Everything is *alucinación*."

Overwhelmed with advice, I left El Ateneo empty--handed. Ben wasn't impressed. What was I—a pilgrim?

In truth, lovers of bookshops can be much like pilgrims; sometimes a shop has a hallowed reputation, and we travel in the hope of a salvific moment. To Paris's Shakespeare and Company, the late George Whitman's tribute to the bookshop of that name run by Sylvia Beach, who published James Joyce's *Ulysses*. To the Bertrand in Lisbon, which opened in 1732 and moved to its present site in Rua Garrett after the original shop was destroyed in the great earthquake of 1755. To Selexyz Dominicanen, which inhabits a thirteenth-century church in Maastricht and used to serve as a peculiarly majestic bike-shed. To the now-defunct Rizzoli on New York's West 57th Street, with its dramatic chandeliers and bas-reliefs, or Tokyo's Morioka Shoten, which at any given time stocks multiple copies of just one book. To Hay-on-Wye at the border between England and Wales, a town of 1,500 souls that has two dozen bookshops and each year briefly swells to accommodate fifty times that number of people as it hosts its famous festival, once described by Bill Clinton as "the Woodstock of the mind".

For most of us, though, the richest bookshop epiphanies have happened not in places to which we traipsed like pious seekers, but in ones we stumbled on.

I'm twenty-three, and I am in Rouen, birthplace of Gustave Flaubert. I first encountered Flaubert through Julian Barnes's novel *Flaubert's Parrot*, which is narrated by a cranky retired doctor, Geoffrey Braithwaite, who is obsessed with accumulating trivia about the writer in a bid "to anatomize the processes of human identity". The day after drinking too many Belgian beers in one of Rouen's rowdier bars, I'm fit to anatomize only the livid rhythms of my hangover, but I buy a copy of Flaubert's *Madame Bovary*. The shop is small and brown and wears the odour of yesterday's cigarettes, and dust sits stubbornly on top of every volume; in short, I'm in the land of cliché, and the tight-lipped owner looks as if she could play one of the Thénardiers in *Les Misérables*—not barrel-like Madame, but rickety Monsieur. The price of my find is ludicrously modest. It's the pale yellow Gallimard edition, and I treat it like treasure, carrying it off to a café where I order a restorative Badoit and begin to read. I've coveted this particular edition of *Madame Bovary* since I saw it in Grant & Cutler in London, maybe six or seven years ago. The book has a military stiffness that suggests it's designed to be read many times. I feel mature and serious simply because I have it in my hands. My very own copy. And never mind that the people at neighbouring tables are rolling their eyes—*Voici un touriste prétentieux!*

In an essay on his life as a bibliophile, Julian Barnes recalls the period in his teens when he discovered "the excitement and meaning of possession": "To own a certain book—one you had chosen yourself—was to define yourself." More than that, it seems to me, to choose a book and take custody of it is a small enlargement of one's self. Many of us cherish libraries, which are on the whole wonderfully democratic institutions and often the wellspring of ideas, but it is on our own bookshelves, packed with our purchases, that we find the archives of our desires, enthusiasms and madnesses.

I'm thirteen, and I accompany my English teacher to a local shop—a place that in my mind is the same shade of blue as a robin's egg—to select some books suitable for handing out at end-of-term prize-giving. The idea is that I'll help him choose titles my schoolmates may actually want, rather than the sort of austere tomes that are usually dispensed on this occasion. Scanning the display of new hardbacks, I'm thrilled to find that some previous browser has slipped into their midst a book called *Merde*, full of "the real French you were never taught at school". No kidding. As I gobble up the unfamiliar racy phrases, I do a dreadful job of selecting books for the prizewinners, and I can't shake my puzzlement—remember, I'm thirteen—at the presence in *Merde*'s section about sex of *une nuit blanche*, meaning "a sleepless night".

Absurd as it may sound, that was a critical moment in my becoming interested in language—in slang, and in the intriguingly disparate slangs of different languages. A bookshop accident launched a lifelong passion.

It's this phenomenon that Mark Forsyth addresses in his essay "The Unknown Unknown: Bookshops and the Delight of Not Getting What You Wanted". When we shop online it's easy to find what we want, yet, when it comes to books, "it's not enough to get what you already know you wanted. The best things are the things you never knew you wanted until you got them". "A desire satisfied," reflects Forsyth, "is a meagre and measly thing. But a new desire!"

Bookshops are forever producing new desires, and they are forever seeding desires in us that will lie dormant for a long time and then suddenly germinate. This is their magic:

inspiration wafts through us, serendipity wakens unfamiliar cravings, dreams dilate, enlightenment irradiates the soul.

Saša Stanišić's piece in this volume likens the relationship between vendor and reader to a drug user's link with his dealer: "One of you has the goods, the other wants a supply of them." Sometimes the book buyer is looking for "the hard stuff that can set off the most complex reactions", and sometimes a fix leaves one with "an impression of convoluted feelings going in all sorts of different directions".

All this mind-altering magic notwithstanding, we live in an age in which bookshops are vulnerable. Their livelihood is under threat from increased rents and rates, as well as from online retail and the allure of jazzier and more aggressively promoted forms of entertainment. An aside: although bookshops are businesses, they are largely exempt from the widespread antipathy to commercialism, partly because they promote literacy and community, but also because they connect us to a past in which retail was less cutthroat and more idiosyncratic.

The essays that follow celebrate the institution of the bookshop; they argue for its value and extol its charm. At the same time, each essay cherishes a particular bookshop or the bookshop culture of a particular place. Here's Juan Gabriel Vásquez on his two favourite spots in Bogotá, both "places of transformation"; and here's Elif Shafak in Kadikoy enveloped by the smells of coffee and linden; and here's Pankaj Mishra in Delhi, carving out a private space for his imagination; and here's Ian Sansom on Charing

Cross Road, unloading new stock at Foyles while the entertainer Danny La Rue descends from his pink Rolls-Royce. Daniel Kehlmann transports us to Berlin's Mitte with its cast of conspiratorial lunchers; Dorthe Nors to rural Jutland and fashionable Copenhagen; and Yvonne Adhiambo Owuor to Nairobi, which is undergoing "a delirium of reconstructive surgery". In some cases the essay is a memorial: Iain Sinclair writes about the defunct Bookmans Halt in St Leonards-on-Sea; Yiyun Li about Beijing's long-gone Foreign Language Bookshop; Stefano Benni about the "dark, mysterious cave" that was La Palmaverde in Bologna.

This is not a gazetteer, a guide to the bookshops of the world. Instead it's an anthology of personal experiences of the book, the most resonant object of the last millennium, and of the special place where readers go to acquire their books—a pharmacy or pharmacopoeia, a miracle of eclecticism, a secret garden, an ideological powder keg, a stage for protest against the banality and glibness of the rest of the world, and also a place of safety and sanity, the only kind of grotto that is also a lighthouse.

Bookshop Time

ALI SMITH

F rom time to time over the past few years I've done volunteer stints a few hours a week selling books at our local Amnesty International second-hand bookshop, Books for Amnesty. I live in a university town in the south of England and the book donations that come in, sometimes seven or eight in a plastic bag, sometimes a whole vanful, a house clearance, someone's whole library, are endlessly interesting, tend towards the eclectic and are almost always unexpected repositories of the lives they've been so close to.

Open this copy of *Ballerinas of Sadler's Wells* (A. & C. Black Ltd, 1954) with its still bright-orange-after-six-ty-years cover and its black and white photo of Margot Fonteyn on the front, its original price of six shillings on the back (now selling at £2). In blue ink on its first page, in neat child's handwriting: *Christmas 1954 To Caroline From <u>Christopher</u>*. Tucked in beside this there's a postcard of a swaggering tabby cat wearing a collar, and written on the back of it in an adult hand in faded blue, *DARLING CAROLINE, <u>PLEASE</u> do send me a list of things you would like to have so that I can have some help to find <u>YOU</u> a birthday present. I shall be stopping at LIZZIE'S next week so please tell Nannie that my address will be Trumpeter's House. Lots of love xx from Mamma xxxxx I thought Papa's present from you lovely.*

Or inside *The Book of the Art of Cennino Cennini* (Allen and Unwin, 1930) a ticket, single, dated 20th July 1936, Chatham and District Traction Company.

Or inside an American first edition of *The Buck in the Snow* by Edna St Vincent Millay (Harpers and Brothers, 1928) a business card for Miss Katzenberger's Piano Lessons and an address in Queens, New York.

We leave ourselves in our books via this seeming detritus: cigarette cards with pictures of trees or wildlife; receipts for the chemist; opera or concert or theatre tickets; rail or tram or bus tickets from all the decades; photographs of places and long-gone dogs and cats and holidays; once even a photo of someone's Cortina. Now when I donate books to the shop I have a flick through to make sure that anything tucked into them isn't something I might mind losing.

The volunteers, like the books, are of all ages and all lifewalks. They all have some things in common; they're doing this for nothing, for Amnesty, most of them because they really love books, many of them because they love the shop, and all of them because they're community-minded. It's quiet in there, browsy, passers-by getting out of the rain, regulars who love the place and know that its stock can be curiously timely—it's not unusual to hear someone exclaim out loud at finding just the book she needs or he's been looking for all this time—and the occasional rogue, like the slightly drunk man who chatted to me for a bit at the cash desk then said, as he left: I was actually planning on shoplifting from here but since you're Scottish I won't. I called after him as he went out the door: If you're going to shoplift don't do it from a charity shop, for God's sake. He gave me a wave and a smile through the window.

Here are some of the things he could've lifted that day. A Leonard Woolf novel called *Sowing*, signed inside *Elizabeth from Leonard, Christmas 1962* (the Leonard who wrote it?). Another Leonard, a biography of Bernstein, definitely signed by the actual Leonard himself in a sloping hand. A copy of Axel Munthe's *The Story of San Michele*, signed and dedicated by Munthe *to Lady Astor*. A ragged copy of *A Girl Like I* by Anita Loos, in which someone has scrawled in claw-hand on the first page, *pArts Of tHis boOk are VERy sAD*.

For every book I donate myself—and this is the problem with a shop like this—a new-bought old book or two, or three or four, tend to come home with me. So much for culling. But what can you do, when you pick up *Hunter's Guide to Grasses, Clovers and Weeds*, 1978 (now £3); flick through it and find out that there are kinds of grass called Timothy and Lucerne, that Timothy came from the US in the 1720s, and Lucerne can't be hurt by drought because its roots go so deep? Or 1964's *National Rose Society Selected List of Varieties* (now £2.50); open it at any page and look what happens: *Oberon, Ohlala, Old Pink Moss, Opera. Ophelia. Optimist, the*. The entry after *Optimist, the*, simply says: "See *Sweet Repose*".

My favourite find so far has been a copy of Lawrence's *Birds, Beasts and Flowers*, not worth much in money terms, apparently, being a second edition. But open it and on its first page someone's stuck a photograph, a young woman in a bathing suit sitting in long grass by the bank of a river, looking in a mirror to do her make-up. Above it, in black ink, in a sweeping hand, *F.N.LW. from P.A. Sept. 1933*. The first bit of the book has been well-read. The later pages are still uncut.

Then there's the *Frescoes from Florence* exhibition catalogue 1969, an Arts Council publication covering the late 1960s European tour. This book, I'd noticed, comes in quite regularly. It always sells. When I saw the third or fourth copy come in I picked it up and leafed through it at the desk. "As is explained by Professor Procacci in his introduction, the removal of these frescoes often laid bare the underdrawing, or sinopia, beneath." I opened it at a page where there was a description of a sinopia in which a woman was holding a small boy by the hand, "later eliminated by the artist, who painted over that portion".

The restorers uncovered him, invisible for centuries, and there all along.

All the years I was growing up, Melvens was the only bookshop in Inverness. It did a roaring trade in tourist books, books about the Jacobites and Mary Queen of Scots, books with "the Surgeon's Photograph" of the Loch Ness Monster on the cover. My father's electrical goods shop was about two minutes away, and when I was a small child I used to hang around Melvens trying not to be noticed, the afternoons between school and the end of the working day when I was waiting for a lift home in the car. It was pointless to pretend to be a bona fide customer when you're only eight, have no money and anyway everyone working in the shop knows you're Smith the electrician's youngest girl, in here again.

Still, I managed to read a lot of books without getting thrown out. *Ghosts and Hauntings*: it was full of real photographs of real ghosts! The book about the Brahan Seer, the ancient man who could see the future through a little hole in a stone he kept in his pocket, who foresaw the Clearances and the Second World War and the coming of the oil industry. He foresaw the infidelity of the husband of his patroness, the rich woman up at the big house, but when he told her about it she was so angry she rolled him down a hill in a burning barrel of tar, but not before he'd foretold the tragic downfall of her whole family and all its descendants, and flung his stone into the sea with the prediction that only a strange and misshaped child of the far future would ever find it again. *Highland Folk Tales*: like the one about the man who killed his friend so he could steal his money, and buried the body under a big stone at the side of the road, then years later was eating his dinner with a set of cutlery whose handles were made of bone, and the bones he held in his hands began to speak, *we are the bones of the friend you killed*, they said, and he looked down and his hands were covered in blood.

But *this isn't a library*—even the nicer woman who worked there had to chase you by saying it, it was her job, and books were dear, I mean expensive. Though that they were dear with the other meaning of dear was clear to me too because of the way my mother and father respected books. Money's never wasted on a book, my mother'd say. One of the very few things that she'd kept with her from her childhood all the centuries back was a small blue book marked with the stamp of the school she attended till her father died and she had to leave to go out to work, *Rip Van Winkle*, about the man who falls asleep for a hundred years. That book, with her name on it from before she'd married our father, was tucked at the back in her wardrobe in behind the clean rows of shoes, and one sunny June afternoon when I was nine, recovering from a bad case of mumps and had been off school for three weeks, she sent me up town by myself to test how well I was, by giving me five shillings and telling me to buy whatever I wanted with it in Melvens.

The special aura of the new-owned book, the healthy shine and promise of it: as I came into adolescence, lucky for me Melvens opened a new downstairs room full of poetry and fiction, which is where I bought my first Lawrence, Mann, de Beauvoir, Hardy, Spark, Dickinson, Stevie Smith, the bright bright orange of Plath's *Johnny Panic*, the L.P. Hartley trilogy about the people with the ridiculous names, and where I first understood that bookshops were also something to do with a differently layered understanding of who you might be, since the people who knew me a bit from life in general, or knew my mother and father or sisters and brothers, but then saw me browsing by myself downstairs in Melvens, regarded me differently afterwards—very like one of the girls in the year above me at school had started treating me differently when she worked out that I didn't just know who Joni Mitchell was, but that I knew all the lyrics off the *Blue* and *Court and Spark* albums—and though I knew immediately it was a sort of snobbery, well, it was one I rather liked.

My English teacher caught my eye one day on the way out of class. There's a shop opened in town I think you'll like, she said. She told me there was a new second-hand bookshop, in a small room up the staircase next to the Market Bar.

My mother looked aghast when I told her. The Market Bar! she said. I'm not going to a bar, I said. It's a *shop*. It's called Leakey's.

The smell of paperback ink and paper was its own intoxication. The books seemed to tower higher than the room. I went, and so did most of the money I earned on a Saturday, £10 a day working in the restaurant at Littlewoods where the other Saturday girls made fun of me for spending my pay packet on so many books every week, and the full-time women were unexpectedly kindly about my being so bookish. *What did you get this time?* John Wyndham. H.G. Wells. Joseph Conrad. Epictetus. Turgenev. Graham Greene. Anything. Everything. A thick green Tennyson collection I saw on the shelf in there one day then had a dream about that night; I told my mother about the dream the next morning. Here, she said to me the next time I was going across town, holding out a note, her purse open in her hand. Buy that book you dreamed about.

I still have most of the books I bought at Leakey's, which had moved from its staircase to a riverfront store many times the size of the narrow room, and happens right now to be one of Inverness's true attractions, one of Scotland's largest collections of second-hand books and maps, and a stunning and welcoming and balconied book-lined paradise with a huge log-burning stove at the heart of it, the promise of something warm to eat always in the air, still at home nearly forty years on in a huge converted church tucked behind the river bank.

I remember reading a piece by Larkin where he writes about how—forgive my paraphrase—if you allocate every ten years of lived life, say, to a weekday, say Monday is the first day of the week and it goes from nought to ten years, and Tuesday from ten to twenty, and Wednesday from twenty to thirty, and so on—then an understanding of where we are in a life will produce a pretty sober vision of the weekend. Myself I've gone from one end of the country to the other and from Monday to Saturday—and I'm still spending my Saturday money in Leakey's. A couple of years ago I was searching for a copy of George Mackay Brown's first collection of poems and I filled in one of those online *alert me* forms in case one ever turned up, though I wasn't that hopeful—1954, quite rare, very slim, paperback, not very many published. Late one evening—ping—an email in the inbox. *The Storm. George Mackay Brown. Seller: Leakey's Bookshop, Church St, Inverness.*

I bought it immediately. Mr Leakey, with whom I have, for forty years, been on polite nodding terms but with whom I've never spoken much more than a hello, a thank you and a goodbye, sent me this email back from his bookshop—one of the best bookshops of my life, now one of the best in the world. *The decades are piling up around us,* he wrote. And *it is a nice copy. It falls into that (distressing, large) category of books that one will see once, if one is lucky, but not again.*

May we all have such luck in our bookshops.

Something that Doesn't Exist

ANDREY KURKOV

arina Libanova has a round face and curly blond hair. I don't know how old she is or how old she was when I met her fifteen years ago during my first ever visit to Chernivtsi, in the middle of the Bukovina region in the south-west of Ukraine, where I gave a talk in the intimate surroundings of her little shop Bukinist (from the French word *bouquiniste*, meaning seller of used and antiquarian books). She was about forty-nine then, and she's about forty-nine now. I can just tell. If you've never been to Chernivtsi—and I'm almost 100 per cent certain that you haven't—all I will say is that a hundred years ago the city's bookshops used to sell books in German, Romanian and Yiddish. And the majority of the city's inhabitants spoke German right up to the end of the First World War—it was part of the Austro-Hungarian Empire, after all. When the empire was replaced by the Romanian monarchy, German was superseded by Romanian in terms of both the spoken and the literary language of the city. A great deal has happened since then. The only problem is that the city's history has been chronicled principally by poets. There have always been too many poets in Chernivtsi; prose writers, on the other hand, have always been in short supply. This is still the case today, a quarter of a century after European political history, with its customary audacity and lack of manners, "drove" the city and its inhabitants out of the Soviet Union and into an independent, post-Soviet Ukraine.

I can clearly remember this time of transition to a new order: in 1991, the stark contrast between grocery shops, with their empty shelves and arrogant, ill-mannered employees, and bookshops, where the bewildered staff stood before shelves full of Soviet literature, which was of no use to anyone any more. Bookshops were the first victims of the crisis. They closed meekly and without protest, without even trying to fight for their survival. After the first couple of years of independence following the collapse of the USSR, out of one hundred bookshops in Kiev just ten remained. I was particularly upset about the closure of Poetry—the only shop in the city that sold nothing but collected works of poetry. During the Soviet era, in the late 1970s or early 1980s, I found a book there called *The Ballads of Kukutis*, by the Lithuanian poet Marcelijus Martinaitis. I looked through it, read a few poems and bought it straight away. It cost me 79 kopecks. Or maybe I'm getting my numbers mixed up... Maybe this happened in 1979? Memory is an unreliable thing. Selective memory is different, though. I can still remember several poems from this collection, word for word. The reason I remember them is because at the time I set those I liked best to music and turned them into songs, which I then sang, accompanying myself on the piano. I must have turned at least twenty of these poems by Marcelijus Martinaitis into songs. I still sing a couple of them, even now. I liked the poetry so much that I immediately assumed the author was long dead. It always seemed to be the case: I would discover some poems that I liked and do a bit of research on the author, only to find out that he had died. Always in that order. Which led me to the conclusion that good poetry cannot be written by living authors. So I didn't even bother trying to find out anything about Marcelijus Martinaitis. Then in 2004 I happened to discover that he was, in fact, alive! But I'll come back to that shortly.

For now, let us return to Bukinist, Marina Libanova's bookshop in the centre of Chernivtsi. Originally, before Marina's time, it was just an ordinary Soviet bookshop selling ordinary Soviet books. Then, all of a sudden, the Soviet Union collapsed, shattering into pieces and passing into history. The Soviet Union had ceased to exist but this little shop survived, weathering the crisis more successfully than bookshops in larger cities. Why? Because the crisis was like the "pause" button on a tape recorder or, in more contemporary terms, like the "pause" symbol of a digital music app on the screen of an iPhone or an iPad. Nobody cancelled it by pressing "play". The thing is, a pause in the development of society that is brought about by crisis has certain characteristics. People run out of money, and in order to survive they start selling things they don't need. Then they start selling things they can live without, and then, if the crisis shows no sign of abating, they start reluctantly selling things they would rather not sell at all. Domestic libraries occupied a special place in the Soviet value system; consequently they were viewed as treasured heirlooms for the older generation to bequeath to their children and grandchildren, who were expected to value them as much as the family silver and considerably more than the legacy of a twelve-place dinner set made by the German company Unger & Schilde after nationalization.

Now "unappreciative" descendants, hungry and starving as they were, set about disposing of these libraries that had been passed on to them by their fathers and grandfathers, collected over the years with blind faith and a firm belief in the idea that "books are the source of all knowledge and wisdom".

The more industrious descendants would stand in the street from morning until night, with newspaper or a piece of oilcloth spread out on the pavement before them and masterpieces of world literature arranged on display alongside textbooks on political economy. The less industrious began carrying their books to bookshops and persuading the owners or their staff to take them on commission, on a sale-or-return basis.

This is more or less how the bookshops of the former Soviet Union became European-style second-hand book-shops and Ukraine itself became a second-hand country. Things began looking up for booksellers. Not only because of the sudden influx of a new breed of client—collectors of rare books—but also because their formerly rather dull and uneventful occupation now involved an element of treasure hunting. After accepting books on commission, the first thing the bookseller would do once the owner of the books had left would be to go through every volume page by page, extracting letters, notes, old bookmarks and sometimes even old banknotes. Not every book yielded such surprises, of course, but they were far from uncommon.

This is also how an ordinary bookshop in Chernivtsi, one of at least twenty, was renamed "Bukinist" and became to all intents and purposes the city's main bookshop. Its location on the importantly named Holovna (Main) Street undoubtedly played a part in its popularity, as did the fact that just a stone's throw away, at the end of a side street opposite the shop, was the Chernivtsi Philharmonic Hall. Historically it had always been the case in Chernivtsi that those who enjoyed reading books also enjoyed listening to classical music and, therefore, regularly attended concerts at the Philharmonic Hall. Sometimes they would also attend author events arranged by Marina Libanova at Bukinist, featuring guest writers and poets, but they often ended up standing in the street and listening through the open door. The shop was so small that no more than twenty people could fit inside at any one time. One day, however, somebody who loved both music and books came up with the idea of bringing these two kindred establishments even closer together. With the permission of the senior management, Marina Libanova began holding author events at the Philharmonic Hall—in the café, just five seconds away from the concert hall itself. Occasionally talks were given to the sound of music, if there happened to be a concert taking place on the other side of the thin café wall, but no books were ever signed on the premises of the Philharmonic Hall. When the event was over Marina Libanova would lead the writer or poet and their audience out of this hospitable temple of music and they would all walk down the side street and across Holovna Street, forming a queue for autographs that led into the bookshop.

Last time I was there—it must be five years ago now—I spent two hours following the same route from the temple of music to the temple of books. After giving a talk in the café of the Philharmonic Hall, I signed books for anyone who wanted one and then lingered in Marina's shop for another half an hour. I wanted to browse, to see if I could find another copy of that collection of poetry by Marcelijus Martinaitis—*The Ballads of Kukutis*. The problem was that my enjoyment of this poetry had robbed me of the book itself. I had forced all my friends and acquaintances to read it, hoping to share with them my delight, and eventually somebody liked the book even more than I did. I never saw it again.

I didn't find it on the shelves of Marina's Bukinist either, despite searching for it with dogged determination for at least half an hour, while Marina drank tea and watched me with a barely concealed smile. Once I had given up and sat down to join her with a cup of tea, Marina told me about several characters who lived in the city, at least one of whom had come into the shop on numerous occasions looking for an imaginary book by an author that didn't exist. This got me thinking for the first time about the existence of such eccentric urban bibliophiles, and I asked Marina more about them. She talked about them kindly, almost affectionately, as though they brought good fortune to the shop or were somehow intrinsically part of the world of books. I remember liking the sound of one individual in particular—a harmless individual who was obsessed with Omar Khayyam. He had been visiting the shop regularly for many years and would always ask Marina if she had anything by Omar Khayyam. If she happened to have one of his books in stock, this gentleman would take it from the shelf and spend ages looking through it. Then he would put it back on the shelf and leave. If not, he would express his disappointment and then leave, but not before asking her to put aside for him the next copy that anyone brought in for resale.

I have looked for *The Ballads of Kukutis* in other bookshops elsewhere in Ukraine, to no avail. Of course I could have looked online, in which case I would almost certainly have found it somewhere out there in the infinite reaches of cyberspace, home to millions of buyers and sellers of everything you could possibly imagine. But Kukutis, like his author Marcelijus Martinaitis, belonged to a different, pre-computer era. His world was not remotely contemporary. The tales he told were of the First World War, of Eastern Prussia going up in flames, of the Lithuanian sky and of his love for the hunchbacked daughter of a miller, whom he hoped to marry. Seeking "access" to the world of Kukutis and his author via the internet felt like sacrilege. And at the end of the day, my stubbornness paid off.

In 2004 my Lithuanian friend Algirdas, who was working in Kiev at the time, bought a white piano and invited me to his house to try out his new purchase. I sang him a few of my songs about Kukutis. Algirdas was astonished, and even more so when he learned the history of my "relationship" with Kukutis. "But he's alive," he insisted, when I told him that I assumed the author had died a long time ago. "Let's give him a call—he's a friend of mine!"

So my friend called Marcelijus Martinaitis on his mobile phone. He asked me to sing my songs about Kukutis and I obliged, accompanying myself on the piano while he held his phone to my mouth. After I'd finished singing I spoke with the creator of Kukutis for the very first time. Marcelijus Martinaitis's voice sounded hoarse, like something from a different world. A person's age is usually reflected in their voice. I learned that Marcelijus liked my songs but his wife Gražina Marija, who was in Vilnius with him listening to my "performance" over the phone, was rather less keen. Nevertheless Marcelijus and I began calling each other regularly, and I would sing to him several times a year. I would always drink a little whisky beforehand, just like I did the first time. I'm still not sure why! Either to improve my singing voice, which has never been any good, or to boost my confidence. I flew to Vilnius a few times in the hope of meeting him face to face, but Marcelijus was often ill and didn't want to see anybody. On the day he died—5th April 2013—I was at home in Kiev with my family, celebrating our daughter Gabriela's sixteenth birthday.

Although I never got to meet Marcelijus himself, I did eventually meet his widow Gražina Marija when I flew out to Vilnius in June that year. She took me to their little house outside the city, where everything had remained just as it was on the day they took him to hospital—as it turned out, his journey's end.

I'm still searching for it, the book that I lost in the early 1980s. *The Ballads of Kukutis*. I look for it the way you look for something you don't really want to find. I call into second-hand bookshops whenever I come across them, several times a year. I ask the staff and they are invariably flummoxed, because they have never heard of this book or its author. After receiving a vague, non-committal reply I inspect all the books on the shelves, or just a few of them if there are too many, and then I leave with a disappointed sigh. I suppose the sales staff might assume that I'm just another eccentric urban bibliophile, looking for a made-up book by a made-up author. But I don't care. It's part of my life. I love second-hand bookshops. I love old books, the musty smell of them and the people who sell them. I love looking for something that I'm never going to find.

I'm sure Marina Libanova remembers me looking for *The Ballads of Kukutis* in her shop too. If she does, she's bound to let me know if a copy ever turns up. Her shop is a veritable cornucopia of rare and interesting books. Books in Romanian and German, published in Chernivtsi, but a hundred years ago, in a different country, when life itself was very different. Books in Belarusian, Ukrainian, Russian and even a few in Yiddish, which was the main language spoken in Chernivtsi for hundreds of years and which, even today, seems perfectly suited to its old alleys and cobbled streets.

What I'm about to tell you now, in conclusion, is highly confidential. But you are a long way from both Kiev and Chernivtsi, so I'm willing to let you in on the secret. In January or February 2013 I asked Marcelijus Martinaitis if he would consider sharing Kukutis with me, if he would permit me to use him as a character in one of my novels—along with his biography, which Marcelijus had been elaborating in poems and ballads over the past fifty years. And he said yes! My novel featuring Kukutis—the eternal Lithuanian with his wooden leg and his love for the hunchbacked daughter of a miller—will be published in a year's time, or thereabouts, and I will have to decide which bookshops and libraries to include on my book tour.

My first port of call will be Chernivtsi, to visit the city's best-known bookshop and its rosy-cheeked, round-faced and curly-haired proprietor Marina Libanova. I'll give a talk in the café of the Chernivtsi Philharmonic Hall, then I'll walk down the side street to Bukinist and sign copies of my novel for anyone who wants one, and then I'll linger for half an hour or maybe longer amongst the pre-loved books. I'll have another look for *The Ballads of Kukutis* and indulge myself once more in the pleasure of feeling like an eccentric urban bibliophile, always searching for something that doesn't exist.

Translated from the Russian by Amanda Love Darragh

The Pillars of Hercules

Ian Sansom

I n 1991 I resigned from my job at Foyles Bookshop on the Charing Cross Road in London. I'd worked there for two years, two years which may or may not have been the happiest two years of my life: it depends on how you look at it; sometimes it can be difficult to tell.

I'd written in on spec, having been drifting aimlessly from job to job, and hardly expecting a reply, but to my surprise I was invited for an interview with Christina Foyle, daughter of the shop's founder. Miss Foyle—everyone called her Miss Foyle—interviewed prospective employees in her luxurious apartment over the shop. (The other pent-house apartment over the shop was owned by the popular female impersonator Danny La Rue, who would sometimes arrive in the loading bay at the back of Foyles in a pink Rolls-Royce, a vision in grey chiffon, and who would call out to us as we were unloading boxes from vans—"Hello Boys!") All I can recall of my job interview is Miss Foyle sitting on a vast white sofa, surrounded by lamps and cushions and cats, and her asking me if I spoke French, to which I replied that I did, although the only French I could and can speak with any degree of confidence are the words "*Je voudrais un sandwich au jambon, s'il vous plaît*", a phrase which had been drilled into us at school in preparation for day trips to France, and which certainly did the job when purchasing filled baguettes in Calais, but which I hardly thought would have passed muster in the Foreign Languages Department of the world's greatest bookshop. Fortunately, Miss Foyle didn't ask a follow-up about my French and I got the job, though not in Foreign Languages; maybe she sensed me bluffing. Over the next few years, working away downstairs, I often thought of Miss Foyle, perched high above us. I would think of Kubla Khan:

> A savage place! As holy and enchanted
> As e'er beneath a waning moon was haunted
> By woman wailing for her demon-lover!

Working at Foyles was not really a career choice; it was supposed to be a stop-gap. The old employment policy ensured that everyone was fired at the end of two years—in order to prevent them gaining any employment rights—but by then most people would already have resigned anyway from boredom, or been sacked for stealing books. I never stole any books myself, being both too timid and also in recovery from a long, draining, intense period of adolescent piety which meant that the mere idea of stealing anything, or of coveting another man's wife, say, or his cattle, was simply unimaginable; I'd have been about as likely to nick the new Philip Roth as to rob a bank. Many of my colleagues, however, managed to combine both a great enthusiasm for literature with the kind of casual unscrupulousness which is common among people in their twenties, who are often more dangerous and unreliable even than teenagers, possessed as they are with the same giddy adolescent drives and desires but also suddenly with the confidence to fulfil them, and they managed to come up with any number of inventive ways of stealing books: some of them used to throw books out of the window to friends waiting down below; others used to just walk straight out the door with the books and sell them directly to the second-hand bookshops located farther down the Charing Cross Road, towards Leicester Square. Mostly, though, they were stealing simply for their own personal use and they'd take the books into the staff toilets, and walk out with them in their bags, or stuffed up their jumpers, and it wasn't just that I thought this was wrong, although I did, of course; it was also that it was unbecoming; as is usual and traditional among ex-religious fanatics, I was gradually transforming from a prig into an aesthete. If there'd been a better, cleaner, more aesthetically pleasing way to steal I might perhaps have been led into temptation.

I liked working at Foyles. I worked in Business and Economics with a middle-aged Czech exile called Henry, which wasn't his real name. He wouldn't tell us his real name: he said it was too difficult for us to pronounce. Henry used to talk about life in Prague before the Communists came, and about Václav Havel, whom he despised, for reasons that I can't now remember: it was either because he was too liberal, or perhaps because he was not liberal enough. Henry was like a mentor to me, the first person I'd ever met in a working environment who I felt I could really respect, the kind of bluff, no-nonsense bloke who taught you about the ways of the world and who told you rude jokes, but who was also intelligent and kind and well-read, and me and Henry and the others in Business and Economics used to spend many happy hours meeting sales reps and cutting open big cardboard boxes of books with sharp knives, and talking about life, the universe and everything, and after work we'd sometimes adjourn to a pub round the corner from Foyles, called the Pillars of Hercules, a pub with all sorts of literary associations—Ian Hamilton had edited his magazines the *Review* and the *New Review* from there, and I'd read about novelists and poets arriving at the pub, clutching their manuscripts to be edited by Hamilton over pints and cigarettes. The Pillars of Hercules was really just your average London boozer but to me it seemed impossibly, fabulously glamorous, even though Hamilton and the *New Review* crowd had long since moved on by the time I arrived, and what I mostly remember about it is being sick in the toilets, and also that it was the first place I saw anybody drink themselves sober.

Henry would often reach a certain point in the evening's drinking where he would be slurring his words and ranting in Czech, and suddenly he'd snap back into consciousness, and into English. It was heroic drinking—totally pointless, and an act of self-harm, but in some way also an assertion of man's free will and dignity. He missed Prague.

Working with Henry in Business was the closest I've ever come to actually working in business and paradoxically it gave me more time to read than ever before (or since). I read business books mostly—books with titles like *Negotiate to Win* and *The Genghis Khan Way of Management*, books whose lessons I never quite seemed to learn. I wasn't the only one. The authors of these books would sometimes turn up unannounced in Business and Economics, to sign copies of their work, or to try to persuade us to take more stock: they were the first authors I'd ever met, and I was shocked and surprised at how dishevelled and desperate they all seemed to be; men in shiny, crumpled suits, with shiny, crumpled faces. I thought authors were supposed to be above it all, like Ian Hamilton in the Pillars of Hercules, or like Henry James and Oscar Wilde, wearing smoking jackets and trading bon mots. I didn't expect them to have business cards and mobile phones, or to try to flog me job lots of their soon-to-be remaindered books. These days, of course, I know better.

Working in Business, I also started to read Czech novelists recommended by Henry—Karel Čapek and Ivan Klíma; and Bohumil Hrabal and Josef Škvorecký. Škvorecký I liked, although I could never pronounce his name, and Čapek I admired. But Hrabal I loved, and have loved ever since. For better and for worse, reading Hrabal made me the writer I am today. I also started to read lots of American novelists I'd never really read before, picking them up from Fiction, down on the ground floor—Donald Barthelme, Cynthia Ozick, Thomas Pynchon, William Gass. I did Updike. I did Roth. I did Bellow. All the usual suspects. I'd spend all day every day—with one weekday and Sunday off—talking with other members of staff, reading, and trying to hide from the customers.

The Business department in Foyles used to be located on the fourth floor, next to Drama & Music and Religion & Philosophy, and I read, or at least browsed, a lot of the books from the shelves all around. This was where I first read Descartes and Richard Rorty, where I first looked at books about jazz and the blues, and where I first discovered William James and Gershom Scholem, and the chord sequences for The Waterboys' *Fisherman's Blues*. I came to regard the shop as my own personal library. It was better than any library there'd been at college: there was no restriction on borrowing rights, and the stock was bang up to date. I used to stack up the books under the till and read them carefully, trying not to break the spines. One of the only things I didn't read much of at Foyles was poetry, which was on the ground floor near the men in suits selling the *Encyclopaedia Britannica*—it was damp and badly lit down there. But I didn't need the half-light of poetry: the world of the fourth floor of Foyles was my oyster. Life was good. Life was sweet.

And then one day my old Economics teacher from school came into the shop. I'd always liked her. Her name was Miss Legan. Once—it was when I was in the fifth form—she'd come into class and told us that she had changed her name and we now had to call her Mrs Koozekhanani. She wrote it on the blackboard. The rumour was that she'd met an Iranian student on the Tube who said he needed a visa, and she'd agreed to marry him. It was certainly possible; she was an extraordinary woman. She wore cords and a donkey jacket, and she had a kind of Joan Baez hairstyle, twenty years after Joan Baez, and she had a National Union of Teachers bumper sticker on her 2CV that read "If you can read this, thank a teacher". She used to give us copies of the *Socialist Worker* to read in class, and she would talk about the miners' strike and the evils of free-market economics. There were also rumours that in the evenings and at weekends she worked as an usherette in the cinema in South Woodford. We were only allowed to study something called "Social" Economics at school—this was a comprehensive school, after all—but Mrs Koozekhanani invited a few of us to learn "Pure" Economics at lunchtime and after school, where she introduced us to the ideas of Karl Marx. In the end, she left—a copy of the *Socialist Worker* too far?—and we got a teacher who wore suits and who preferred Friedrich von Hayek. If we weren't socialists before, we certainly were after.

"What on earth are you doing working here?" Mrs Koozekhanani asked me when we met in Foyles, years later, her hairstyle and cords still intact. "You're wasting your life," she said. "You have a responsibility to yourself and others to do better. You have a contribution to make to society." I thought working in Foyles was my contribution to society.

After leaving school and a few false starts I'd eventually gone to university and studied English. Like most university students of English I'd chosen to do English at degree level because I'd been good at English at school, or at least I liked reading books, and at school these two things—enjoying reading and "doing English"—happily coincide. Of course, the further you go on in education, the more they diverge, until you eventually meet people with doctorates on Abjection in Early Modern Literature who hate reading and who hate writers, and who haven't read a book for pleasure or out of mere curiosity for years. Unfortunately, it's not until you actually go to university and start reading literary theory and literary criticism that you realize your mistake, by which time it's too late. I flirted with the idea of changing to study theology, or art history—something more useful—but in the end I stuck it out with English, despite or perhaps because of the fact that I was told by one supervisor, in my very first term at college, that I was, quote, the most inarticulate student it had ever been his misfortune to teach, unquote. I regarded it—as he probably intended it—as a challenge. I spent three years learning how to punctuate, and ironing the Estuary out of my voice.

After university I got married, travelled around for a while, slipped back into glottal-stopping, gave up on semicolons, did a lot of odd jobs, moved with my wife to Belfast, worked as an adult literacy tutor, and eventually moved back to London. I did a TEFL course while my wife worked as a shop assistant at H. Samuel, the jewellers. For years we were happily going nowhere fast. Then I got the job in Foyles and my wife was accepted on a graduate trainee scheme: things were getting serious; things were looking up.

The great thing about Foyles was you got paid in cash every week in little brown envelopes, so it seemed like a real job, like you were working in a factory or in the shipyard. For the first and last time in my life I felt like I was paying my way. I felt like my dad and my grandad must have felt during their working lives—I felt that somehow I was providing. With commission, you could earn £150–£180 per week, more than I'd ever earned before. At the time, we were living in a one-room flat in Crystal Palace. It was cramped, with one wall partitioned off from the next flat by a sheet of wallpapered hardboard: we could hear when the woman next door used her deodorant; when she entertained male guests we retired to the pub. We ate out occasionally in a cheap Chinese restaurant in West Norwood, went shopping in Brixton and to the cinema in Streatham.

And it was then that Mrs Koozekhanani came along and shook things up and spoilt everything. Maybe she was right. Maybe I was wasting my life. Maybe there was more to life that hiding from customers and reading books at random and pissing away my wages in the Pillars of Hercules.

So I moved on and didn't return to Foyles for years. Then one Christmas I was visiting my family in London and I thought I'd look up Henry in Business and Economics. I went up to the fourth floor and sure enough, there he was, still there, hiding behind the desk, and we went out to the Pillars of Hercules, for old times' sake, just me and him. We talked about books and about the book trade, and he told me about his plans to go back home to Czechoslovakia, and how he was going to set up a factory manufacturing gloves, or maybe beer, or plastics, or something, and I said how good it was to see him again, and he said it was good to see me too, and how we should meet up again soon, and when I got home that night I opened my bag and in there was a big bottle of brandy—he must have bought it at the bar and slipped it in while I went to the toilet. A true act of kindness.

Six months later I moved back to live in London and again went to find Henry, up on the fourth floor, but this time he'd gone. Disappeared. No one working there had even heard of him. I never even knew his real name, and I haven't seen him or heard from him since, and I don't ever expect to. Foyles has gone as well now, of course: it's not the same place. It's moved a few doors down the road

to the old St Martin's School of Art and is now indistin-
guishable from any other fancy bookshop in the city. Long
gone is the strange payment system, with the Soviet-style
double-queuing, and gone too are the big red heavy volumes of *Whitaker's Books In Print*, and there is of course
the obligatory coffee shop, and there are scanners and
computers and a website. Life moves on, and everything
changes, even in the greatest bookshop in the world.

The last time I was in London I took my son for a drink
in the Pillars of Hercules. "This is where it all began," I
said, as we passed the building that once was Foyles, though
what began there I'm not entirely sure—perhaps it wasn't
the beginning at all. Perhaps it was the end.

A Tale of Two Bookshops

JUAN GABRIEL VÁSQUEZ

A t the beginning of 1993, in the middle of a summer of exceedingly blue skies, I went back to university to resume the second year of my law degree. I'd initially been convinced that it was my destiny to be a lawyer, in spite of the fact that what had most interested me since I was a boy, apart from football, were the novels that I read as if my life depended on them. But something happened in those years of civil codes and notes on Roman law. No one knows how a vocation manifests itself, or what paths destiny uses to appear to its victims, but this had happened to me during the transition from one year to the next: I discovered that my passion for novels was not simply a reader's passion, but that I was going to devote my life to trying to write them. I began to skip classes, not just because lessons on contracts or civil procedural law threatened to bore me to death, but because out there in central Bogotá were a handful of bookshops that I began to visit the way a sick man visits his doctor or a delinquent finds his refuge. The one I visited most—the best as well as the closest to the university—was the Librería Lerner.

The Lerner was and remains an establishment with a spacious ground floor; its crammed display windows wrap right around the corner of the block. But it's a curious corner, for the building that houses the bookshop, on Avenida Jiménez, is a sort of ship of magnificent architecture and irregular shapes. Its narrow prow once harboured the offices of the newspaper *El Espectador*, and García Márquez writes in his memoir *Living to Tell the Tale* that every day an employee would lean out of the window to hang up a blackboard with the most important news of the moment written in chalk. That's how people found out what was going on in the world; if they wanted to know more, they'd have to buy the newspaper the next day. Anyway, I passed in front of this illustrious prow with its illustrious past at least three times a week, during the three years or so that went by between my decision to be a novelist and the day in 1996 when (to try to be a novelist) I left Colombia. I walked past the prow of the building, went into the Lerner and, depending on how much time I had, I'd take a quick look around the main floor or go downstairs where I might spend hours sitting on the ground, leafing through the towers of books I'd picked out in order to choose one or several to buy and imagining, as all apprentices do, the moment when one of my own books might be there, on those shelves, ready to be leafed through and perhaps bought by an unsuspecting reader.

Bookshops, for a writer, are places of transformation. When a writer is asked to choose his favourite bookshops, he won't generally pick the one he most often visits, but rather the scenes that inspire his nostalgia: the nostalgia of starting out. He'll remember the tough years when his literary vocation was an unresolved compulsion, because there is no fixed and sure method of turning a novice into a novelist. So, with all the passion of my twenty-year-old self, I went to the Lerner. I tended to get lost among the shelves of the main floor, with lighting that's less than ideal for resting your eyes on the books of others, and think of the miracle of my own book—that book I hadn't even imagined yet, hadn't even begun to write—one day being on those shelves, leaning against its neighbour in alphabetical order: Mario Vargas Llosa. That was when I discovered that the alphabet has its hidden magic, for Vargas Llosa was my maestro and my model in those days: the kind of writer I wanted to be. Years later, the writer Santiago Gamboa confessed to me the profound excitement he experienced when imagining his books beside those of García Márquez, just as they are in bookshops today, and the writer Antonio Sarabia, aware that his main influence was José Saramago, was also delighted to have him as a neighbour. Still today, when I'm visiting one of the cities where I've lived and looking for a Vargas Llosa novel in a bookshop—La Central or Laie in Barcelona, L'arbre à lettres in Paris, Pax in Liège—and see mine leaning against his, I remember those days and am astonished at all that has happened since. This feeling of astonishment is something that certain bookshops give us.

The Lerner had and still has several leather armchairs arranged as if in someone's living room, so we readers can sit down like guests at a big party in a hospitable house. This is the opposite of what happens in so many bookshops these days, where the reader is seen as an intruder who comes in to waste time and might not even buy anything, and where the employees disapprove of the sacred habit of browsing, maybe because they never practised it. There, in those armchairs, I would finish my hours of excursions, trying to choose the right book, which I could allow myself within my student budget. There I decided to buy *The Unbearable Lightness of Being* by Kundera and *The Stranger* by Camus, in cheap Alianza paperbacks; there I leafed through all three volumes of Hermann Broch's *The Sleepwalkers*, but the Lumen editions were too costly in those days, and I had to wait for a charitable soul to give them to me on my next birthday; there I discovered and bought a book of conversations with Adolfo Bioy Casares, *A la hora de escribir* (*When Time Comes to Write*), which awakened the irrational fondness I still have for interviews with writers. The interviewer asked Bioy Casares if he stops living when he's writing. "No," replies Bioy, "I believe it's just the opposite. I dare to advise people to write, because it's like adding an extra room to the house of one's life. There is life and there is thinking about life, which is another way of living it intensely."

A few pages further on, a sentence in my copy is highlighted in green. Bioy is asked about his first literary efforts, which he didn't like. "What I did like was literature," says Bioy. "I felt that it was my homeland and I wanted to participate in its world."

I came up out of the basement of the Lerner (the daylight stung my eyes) and thought that was how it was: that literature was my homeland and I wanted to participate in that world.

I I

Only one Bogotá bookshop competed in those *Bildungsroman* days with the loyalty I had to the Lerner. Seventy-six streets to the north, the Central bookshop was its opposite in every way. On the one hand, it was in a quiet, middle-class neighbourhood, not in the busy city centre, and, although it wasn't small, the whole place would have fitted in the basement of the Lerner. On the other hand, it hadn't been my personal discovery, the way the Lerner had, but a sort of paternal inheritance: my father knew the owners from way back, and for years had been such a faithful customer that he could take books home on credit and pay for them at the end of the month. I inherited that privilege: I don't remember how or when, but one day I began to buy books with nothing but my signature on a sheet of lined paper, and more than once I've had to leave my whole month's earnings in that till having signed for so many books over the course of the month without thinking of the accumulating bill.

The owners of the Central were a Jewish couple from Austria, Hans and Lilly Ungar, who had arrived in Colombia in the inter-war years. In 1947, young Hans frequented a bookshop on the now disappeared Pasaje Santa Fe, a stone's throw from my university. When the owner died, his widow suggested that Hans take over the bookshop, and to achieve this he had to work there and pay off the costs with his modest salary. Several years and locations later, the Central became such an important place for me that it ended up appearing in my novel *The Informers*. The narrator had published a book about the life of Germans—Nazi sympathizers or Jewish refugees—in Colombia at the time of the Second World War. His main source for the book, a woman called Sara Guterman, had just died when we read:

Once the book was published, when I found a message on my answering machine in which Lilly invited me in a formal and rather peremptory tone to come to the bookshop, I thought the invitation was in some way related to Sara Guterman, or, at least, to that never-delivered lecture on the hidden anti-Semitism of Colombian politicians, for Hans Ungar (everyone knew this) was one of the most direct victims of the prohibitions López de Mesa used to minimize the number of Jews arriving in Colombia, and he often said in interviews, but also in casual conversations, that his parents had died in German concentration camps largely due to the impossibility of obtaining a Colombian visa for them such as the one he'd obtained and with which he'd entered the country, from his native Austria, in 1938. So anyway, when I arrived at the appointment I found them both, Hans and Lilly, sitting beside the solid, grey table that functioned as the meeting place for the Germans of Bogotá and from which, with the help of a dial telephone and an old typewriter—a Remington Rand, tall and heavy like a scale model of a coliseum—they ran the bookshop. In the main display cabinet there were three copies of my book. Lilly was wearing a burgundy-coloured turtleneck sweater; Hans was wearing a tie and between his suit jacket and tie he had put on an argyle sweater.

I must have written this at the beginning of 2003. By that time I'd been living outside Colombia for seven years and it would be another nine before I went back, but that doesn't mean I didn't visit my country on holidays; more than once, during those short visits, I went to the Central to make sure things were as I remembered them and as I'd described them. They were—with one exception. The solid grey table remained, as did the typewriter and the telephone from which I had made several urgent calls in the days before cell phones. But in 2004, when I went to the bookshop for the first time since the publication of my novel, Lilly Ungar complained to me of something that her affection did not manage to attenuate. Hans, she told me, had voiced the opinions I used about the anti-Semitism of the Colombian authorities in several interviews in the 1940s, but his opinion had changed over the years, or he'd no longer felt it right to express it in those terms, and I'd been wrong to use a real person in my fiction without asking his permission or giving him the opportunity to control the words I put in his mouth. Lilly was angry, and I was very sorry about that. The conversation ended with a novelist's reprimand:

"And also," she told me, "Hans never wore argyle sweaters."

A lot of time has gone by since that conversation, and the frequency of my visits to the Central has diminished. But I still recall fondly those days of taking books home without paying for them, which gave the purchase a certain feeling of impunity. Thus, one day I took home Alfredo Bryce Echenique's *Complete Short Stories*; I took *Las poéticas de Joyce* (*The Aesthetics of Chaosmos: The Middle Ages of James Joyce*), an academic book by Umberto Eco I read several times, and *Kafka: Towards a Minor Literature*, an academic book by Deleuze and Guattari that I never read. There, in the Central, I bought *Los días enmascarados*, early short stories by Carlos Fuentes (3.100 pesos), and also *Paideia: The Ideals of Greek Culture*, by Werner Jaeger (18.800 pesos). The prices are written in my copies, by hand and in pencil, but I'm not sure in whose hand. Maybe it was the hand of Estela, the woman who awaited me beside the till, either to ask for my signature on the chits of my cashless purchases or to write down my whimsical special orders. These days of online shopping have robbed us of this as well: the peculiar pleasure of not finding the book, having to request it and wait for days or weeks or even months for it arrive. The immediate satisfaction of online buying is no fun for me. Visiting several stores in search of a book, tracking it down and hunting for it like a difficult prey, continues to be one of the pleasures that is turning me, bit by bit, into an anachronistic bibliophile.

In my novel, the narrator sits down in front of a grey table and begins to sign a pile of copies of his own recently published book. I've never done that at the Central, but I still give myself the secret satisfaction of occasionally returning to the bookshop and confirming my books are there, between Vargas Llosa and Vázquez Montalbán, and I still enjoy knowing the layout of the shelves and location of the books that interest me, and I still regret not being able to speak German so as to read the books Hans displayed on a special table, at the back and to the right, like the unclaimed letters of a lost country. And I remain full of admiration for this place, between the walls of which I've found so much happiness in print, and grateful that it is still alive and still in the hands of the Ungar family, seventy years on, instead of having sunk under the competition from the internet, which treats books as if they were hairdryers, or from so many contemporary readers, traffickers of electronic files for whom literature is so important, but so important that it doesn't seem fair to them to pay for it.

My favourite bookshops have changed with the years and my travels and needs. But these two, the Lerner and the Central, remain alongside the new ones that keep opening in Bogotá: the Madriguera del Conejo (the Rabbit's Warren), for example, or Wilborada. What I look for in them is always the same. The best bookshops are meeting places, spaces for cultural exchanges and for belonging to that mysterious world Bioy Casares had in mind when he said that literature was his homeland; and nevertheless, a bookshop is (as well, at least for me) a place where I can be alone in a solitude I can't find anywhere else. I go to my favourite bookshops—from the Strand in New York to El Virrey in Lima, by way of Daunt Books in London—to while away time in solitude and, in that lost time, to find something. A good bookshop is a place we go into looking for a book and come out of with one we didn't know existed. That's how the literary conversation gets widened and that's how we push the frontiers of our experience, rebelling against its limits. This is something else online commerce deprives us of: on a website we cannot discover anything, we can't bump into the unexpected book, because an algorithm predicts what we're looking for and leads us—yes, mathematically—only to places we already know.

So, you see, bookshops have been an inextricable part of my life as a novelist. Not just because I discovered my masters there, but because my life as a novelist could be portrayed in a series of bookshop tableaux. I can think, for example, of the day in 1997 when I arrived at the Librería Española in Paris, a legendary place on the rue de Seine, with seven copies of my first and forgotten novel. I left them there on consignment; I returned a month later to find they'd all been sold. (La Librería Española, founded by Republican exiles, outlived Franco by several years, but did not survive the internet.) I can also think of the bookshop in Hay-on-Wye where I found a volume, gathering dust, that contained letters written from Colombia by an American Peace Corps volunteer. That book—published privately and discovered on the unpredictable shelves of a second-hand bookshop—turned out to be a key document for me when I was writing *The Sound of Things Falling*. The best bookshops are places where the principle of serendipity, which in broad strokes consists of finding the book you need when you don't yet know you need it, presents itself in all its splendour. A reader's life is, among other things, this tissue of opportune coincidences.

Translated from the Spanish by Anne McLean

Leitner and I

SAŠA STANIŠIĆ

H ello, my name is Saša, and I'd like to tell you about Leitner.

Hello, Saša.

I was new to the city, and distrustful; I thought I might easily come up against a know-it-all in that environment, or a show-off, or even worse, someone whose stuff just wasn't to my taste. But I had to find someone I could trust in future, because who likes changing his dealer?

No one.

Exactly.

In our line of business, you need trust more than mutual liking. One of you has the goods, the other wants a supply of them. Things get critical only if your wishes aren't clear—if you don't know just what you need—and that's the case with me most of the time. I may know the kind of effect that I want, but not the actual name of the substance.

And I also felt ashamed, even after moving to the new city, of confessing yet again to myself and a stranger that yes, I did have supplies of my own at home, I even have my own laboratory where I make such things myself, but still it isn't enough, I need new stuff too. Or very old stuff; my preferences vary.

Most of all I was afraid of being asked whether I had tried a shot of this or that classic fix, because I very seldom had. That's bad. And I also had to convey my dislike of being in shops. I'd agreed with Leitner's predecessor that I could visit his place before and after opening times. Proximity to other users intimidated me. I wanted to be alone in making my choice; there's hardly anything more intimate.

I can understand that.

Thanks, Jürgen.

On the other hand, wouldn't Leitner, intent on acquiring me as a regular customer, also have to show his best side? After all, as everyone knows, his profession is a risky one.

That's terrible!

Yes.

More and more people are clean these days, or they get what they need in other ways. I must admit that, in the transitional phase of my move to a new city, I'd tried getting a quick fix straight from the manufacturer. Once I even resorted to the major distribution channel so much feared by independent middlemen. It sold me good stuff, no question, but I can't deny that I was uneasy about it.

I know the feeling.

I felt I was letting someone down, but at that time I didn't yet know the someone concerned—Leitner.

It was he who made contact with me in the end. He said he would like to organize a little sales event for me, so that I could introduce my own substances to his customers. Generous of him, don't you think?

Wow.

You see, I've tried my hand at manufacturing substances, and there are three of mine on the market. Some people like them, others don't. That's life.

I like the first one. It goes down really well.

Thanks, Johanna.

Really well.

Thanks.

Selling them myself, though—that was beyond me. I didn't feel at ease pushing them on the market. So many novelties, year after year, and in among them all: me, wandering around like a taxi driver in a big city who knows his way up and down only three streets.

Leitner invited me to introduce my own stuff in his shop. It was the end of the month, my finances were running low, I had to be glad of any takers, so I accepted the invitation.

His handshake was perfect. Not too firm, not too limp. It was obvious that I'd have to watch out. You don't play games with people who have a perfect handshake. They've shaken countless hands to achieve that perfection.

I arrived a little late, and we went straight to a juice bar next door, where we each had a juice made from fruits with unpronounceable names. Leitner conspicuously avoided all subjects that could lead to the discussion of substances. He doesn't want to pester me, I thought. I'd have been glad if things were the other way around and he'd wanted favours from me. Maybe he distrusted me himself. Maybe he wanted to hear how I talked about my own stuff before showing me what he had to offer.

I decided to get through my presentation and then disappear quickly. I didn't want anything to do with a man who had a handshake like that and acted as if the business didn't interest him.

His shop was well filled. There were friends there, regular customers, and the passing trade too. I offered a few samples of my own production, and was rewarded with polite appreciation. We ended the evening with a glass of wine.

Leitner is a clean-shaven man, only a few years older than me, always moving around in front of his shelves in jeans and shirt, and not even proud, it seemed, of owning so much of the stuff. Rather shy and withdrawn, even in conversation.

I surreptitiously looked round. He was openly offering hundreds of substances for sale. As well as the hard stuff that can set off the most complex reactions in the user, there were items like *Faust* that have been compulsorily handed out to schoolchildren for decades now.

The best-known Austrian manufacturer, Bernhard, had a whole shelf to himself. His substances didn't go down well with everyone, being rather hard to digest and liable to set off a distaste for your own country as a side-effect, especially if that country was Austria.

Some substances were exhibited in full view in the middle of the shop. Most of the manufacturers were unknown to me. Fashionable phenomena, I assumed, bestsellers that created a great stir on the market and then soon disappeared. I was a little disappointed. As I saw it, a good dealer didn't need to sell modish junk.

A second glance told me that I'd been ignorant, and confirmed that I didn't know anything about selling. These were indeed little-known substances from little-known manufacturers, but hardly any of them were new to the market. This was where Leitner and his pushers displayed their own favourites, each accompanied by an additional note listing its effects and side-effects, thus making it easier for clueless users like me to choose.

I suddenly felt the dealer's hand on my arm. I'd had the feeling anyway that he was watching me, as if waiting for his moment to act. Now he struck, directing my attention to a substance promising "a new kind of experience of the animal kingdom". He tapped it and said, "Suits your character."

The substance was called *Esel* (which means "Donkeys").

I was baffled. I did like donkeys, but they're not exactly famous for their positive characteristics. All the same, I was impressed that a man whom I'd known only for an evening would be so forthcoming with me.

I said I'd buy the substance. He waved to a young woman who led me to an old-fashioned till at the back of the shop. I hesitated, making out that I'd changed my mind. When I came to the front of the shop again, Leitner wasn't there.

The next day there was a paper bag containing some old gear outside my door. Shakespeare. Nothing unusual about that, and no risk; I had several Shakespeares in stock, but I had never entirely developed a taste for it. I preferred substances that took effect quickly. With Shakespeare I couldn't shake off an impression of convoluted feelings going in all sorts of different directions, unnecessarily entangled and hazy.

On closer examination, it turned out to be a rare variant made in Germany, a 1923 version of *Romeo and Juliet*. In spite of its age, it was in good condition. In the U-Bahn I allowed myself to sample a couple of lines. They were excellent, and the outward appearance of my fix also pleasantly distinguished it from the e-substances being taken by my fellow travellers.

A business card told me that the gift had come from Leitner. Beside his email address, he had written: *If there's anything else you need…*

This was the meeting I was afraid of. The one that would take place after I first called Leitner because I *needed something*. He hadn't suggested his shop as the meeting place. The stuff he offered for sale there was certainly good, and some of it unusual. But with the perfect Shakespeare that I enjoyed line by line in the course of the week, he had shown me what was really possible. Furthermore, his shop was at the other end of town.

A week later the effect of *Romeo and Juliet* had worn off, and I took a quick fix of Kehlmann, a substance mysteriously entitled *F* that turned me, while the effect lasted, into a deceiver, a swindler, an illusionist.

But I wanted pure emotions. I remembered the strong feelings of shame, hatred and happiness that the cocktail of substances entitled *Dating Miss Universe* had aroused in me a few years ago. "Leg" had been the name of one of the ingredients. I wanted to taste the rest of the cocktail. But online research showed that the substance was prohibitively expensive in its hard form, and the soft variant was difficult to find. The name of the manufacturer was Steven Polansky.

Then I thought of Leitner. I sent him an email saying what I wanted. I told him the online price, adding that I wouldn't be able to pay that much. He'd be asking at least the same, I thought, and I liked the idea of putting him in a tight spot.

Why?

Good question, Jürgen. I don't know.

Leitner's answer came straight back. "No problem. Monday? Where?"

It was as if he'd just been waiting for my request. I was startled, but of course I couldn't go back on the deal now. I suggested a coffee shop near my apartment, early in the morning so that the whole thing would look like a meeting between two acquaintances before work.

He was waiting for me, with a black coffee in front of him, the paper bag beside him and in it, of course, the gear he had brought me.

"Not so simple, was it?" I said.

"It depends what you mean by simple," he replied, pushing the bag over the table.

I risked glancing inside. It was indeed the hard version of Polansky's *Dating Miss Universe*. The bill was with it. He was asking only a fraction of the online price.

"How did you manage that?" I asked.

"The other one's on the house," said Leitner, instead of answering me.

Sure enough, there was more gear in the bag. *The School for Fools*, by a manufacturer called Sokolov.

The name meant nothing to me. And how on earth did Leitner know that I spoke Russian?

Directly after that meeting, when we said not another word about business, I went home, drew the curtains over the window and inhaled *The School for Fools* from beginning to end. I still think of it as one of the best trips I ever had in my life. A wild, anarchic experience that transferred me to a deeply Russian frame of mind, a trip full of symbols and signs and fine irony.

And how uncanny, for heaven's sake, was Leitner? A man who knew his customer's habits so well after a single meeting—where do you find that kind of thing these days? Spoiling the customer by giving him presents, keeping his interest going with little surprises. I could see through the method, but I thought: this is great—I like presents and surprises.

I was already giving Leitner my next order. "Something like Sokolov, but from the USA?"

This time the answer was some while in coming. Just as I feared that my wish had been presumptuous or too vague, Leitner sent me a list of substances from ten manufacturers, one from each, with no further comments. It began with a name I knew: Barry Hannah. The following names, too, were familiar to me. I had something by every one of them in the room where I keep my supplies. But I didn't know the particular substances enumerated by Leitner. It was as if, with the contents of my shelves before his eyes, he had been completing my collection.

Under the list he wrote, "Where and when?"

Once again we met early at the coffee shop. Once again he had brought the stuff in a paper bag, and once again the price was almost too good. I had ordered the first three on the list, sight unseen. Number four was Leitner's last free gift. Now that I'd fallen for him, he didn't need to make me any more presents.

That morning he left quite soon. Looking through the window, I watched him go: jeans, shirt and a backpack, an inconspicuous man holding his phone, speaking briefly into it, putting it away again, and then he had disappeared from my field of vision.

*　　*　　*

Exactly a year has passed since our first meeting. I've never been in his shop again. Instead, I enjoy the exclusive attentions of a personal dealer who has the nerve to persuade me not to buy substances if he isn't sure of their effect. When I asked him for *Purity*, his answer was to send me a link to a YouTube video over seven minutes long, showing an old propeller aircraft failing to take off.

I thought I'd like to tell you about my dealer.

I'm not new here now, and I am still distrustful. I don't know anything about him. True, Leitner did once tell me he's married and has two children, but then next time he sold me a substance that immersed me in images of an unhappy marriage, as if to say: it doesn't matter who I am, only the substance counts.

Once I asked what his own fix is. He looked genuinely surprised that I wanted to know. He spoke hesitantly, as if afraid it would lose some of its effect if he described it to me. It was strange stuff. Strange to me. It included Danielewski. I got hold of that myself, tried the first pages and put it aside, disturbed.

I'm still waiting for him to put a foot wrong. Week after week we meet early in the morning, week after week I'm not disappointed: McCarthy, Ruff, Saunders. Ahrens, Benn, Atwood.

I ask you, is there anything better than a dealer who can get you to consume more and more of his stuff?

Yes, how about spring?

Thanks, Johanna, that's true.

Life is too short for bad trips. As they say. My dealer would never say that. My dealer hates platitudes. His answer is: "When and where?"

In a paper bag: language, courage, magic. A bit of Cheever, a touch of Claire Keegan, and the first volume of *Game of Thrones*.

In spring I'm going to retreat into privacy and consume them all one after another. What better habit could I have?

Translated from the German by Anthea Bell

All that Offers a Happy
Ending Is a Fairy Tale

Yiyun Li

T his is a fairy tale about a bookshop, and to tell the story I have to start long before the bookshop came into my life. In the beginning I did not know there was such a thing as a bookshop. I knew books, and bookshelves. Our family and families around all had bookshelves—they were the same size, dark brown, issued, along with other furniture, by the research institute where my father worked as a nuclear physicist. We had been assigned two bookshelves, one claimed by my grandfather, who shared a bedroom with my sister and me and whose books were stitched bound, their pages yellow and flimsy—these he had accumulated throughout his scholarly and editorial career, though I understand now it would be more accurate to say that these books had been rescued from a downward journey from an editor and scholar to an almost-enemy of the state. (He and his two sons had fought against the Communist army in the civil war.) On the other bookshelf were books from my parents' youths. There were Russian textbooks and treasures—one of them, I was told, was Lermontov's *A Hero of Our Time*, which my parents used as a photo album with many finger-sized, black and white pictures of people from before they were married and had children. There were my father's textbooks from university on classical mechanics and quantum physics. There were a handful of books that I had read and reread during elementary school: revolutionary novels (*The Golden Road*, *The Tale of Red Flag*, *The Bright Sunny Day*), Gorky's autobiography, *The Gadfly* by Ethel Voynich. (The last of these I could almost memorize in parts; there were a few illustrations, exotic but pretty, of Catholic priests, dark confessionals and a young man butterfly-hunting in an Italian valley; there was a picture of Voynich herself, her Irish face equally foreign.)

Other families had books, too, mostly the same ones, though in second grade a friend discovered a copy of *Arabian Nights* on her parents' bookshelf. It was the first children's book—or so I believed it to be—that I had encountered, and I convinced the friend to lend it to me. Three days, she had me promise, and I devoured the book in three days, thrilled by the threat of impending execution but also confused by the abundance of cucumbers and naked people.

In the beginning it did not occur to me to ask from where the books had come onto people's bookshelves. Of course I'd seen new books, in a department store near us, though it would be more accurate to call it a general store. Everything was kept behind counters, and one had to ask a shop assistant—the most impatient people you would ever meet, if you grew up in Beijing in the 1970s and 1980s and knew the shop assistants as I did—to see a pair of shoes, a roll of fabric, a blouse, or a water kettle. On Sundays, which was the only weekend day, the store was packed. When I read in fiction now about a crowded bar—"three or four deep"—I see the tiny department store. It was a battle to get the attention of a shop assistant, and a lost battle if you dared to ask to see alternatives.

The book department was not as crowded, and sometimes my parents left me there while they pushed through the crowds to fill the shopping list. It was a hopeless affair to watch the books from a distance, as they were either in the glass cases or on the shelves behind the counter. I did not have money. The books, I understood without being yelled at, were to be paid for before being touched.

One had to look elsewhere for reading material. We lived on the ground floor of an apartment block, and twice a day the postman delivered mail into a green, wooden box, which did not have a lock, next to our door. Newspapers, on subscription, arrived daily. Postcards, drably coloured and issued by the postal service, came regularly—it was cheaper to send a postcard than a letter. Because I was a perpetual loiterer by the mailbox, and because I could retreat at the first sign of danger, I read the newspapers and postcards when they came in. I read envelopes too, memorizing the senders' names and addresses and making up words for what would be in the letters. A letter had to have a good reason for being written. My grandmother—my father's mother—wrote once a year. Unusually for her generation of village women, she could write beautifully, though her husband, a poor peasant from the mountain, was completely illiterate—one of those people who would have to press a red-inked thumb on any official paper rather than signing his name. Of course I read my grandmother's letters, too; I knew where my father kept them in a neat stack. It always started with this old-fashioned greeting: *Ling-Zhi, mine son, seeing this letter is as seeing mine face.* Ling-Zhi was my father's milk-name, used by my grandmother only. That he had a mother was a renewed surprise when I reread her letters. She spoke of her pigs and her chickens in the letters, and of my father's younger siblings, some of whom he had barely known because he had left home at ten to seek an education. He was the first one in his village to go to a university, and it was said that his mother could only afford a pair of socks, so the villagers had pooled the money to buy a suitcase. He had travelled from southern China to the north with a pair of socks in an empty suitcase.

If you were like me, you would know the obsession of the compulsive reader: every street sign; every bottle label; the newspaper wrapping the fish and dripping liquid; the soles of new shoes; decades-old slogans printed on abandoned houses; the daily expenses my father recorded in a notebook. On a bus you would memorize the serial number and manufacturing date of the seat in front of you. In the hallway of the paediatrics department you would sneak to the registration desk and look at the names and ages printed on the medical records of all those coughing children. In third grade when I had measles and was quarantined for three weeks at home, I finished the *Complete Manual of Barefoot Medics*. It was published in 1969, a thick volume of eight hundred pages, with almost all the diseases possible or beyond imagination, with gruesome descriptions and even more gruesome illustrations. When you have measles you are not supposed to read or watch television (we didn't have a set, in any case) or open the curtain to see the daylight: the eyes of a measles-afflicted child are easily destroyed if care is not taken. This last fact I both read in the barefoot medics' manual and understood through my own experience: my parents had taped a piece of fabric onto the bookshelf to keep all books unavailable, but they had left the medical manual at large, which was constantly used as a guide to my recovery. I lost my good eyesight after the measles; it's one thing that's been all the way downhill since then.

No, I was not the Sleeping Beauty. I would never close my eyes if a book were within reach.

The profession I fantasized about was not a bookshop owner as you might imagine (even if I'd discovered what a bookshop was), or the shop assistant behind the book counter. Not every Cinderella wants to go to the ball. Rather, my dream was to become a postwoman. Once my grandfather and I walked past the district post office in the afternoon. After a beep, the gate opened and more than a hundred postmen and postwomen rode their green bicycles out, all bells clanging, all mailbags on their crossbars plump. I didn't know how to ride a bike then—I was a bookish child with an awkward ten-year-old body—and it had become clear to me that to learn to ride a bicycle was imperative to my happiness: imagine all the postcards and newspapers and envelopes that I could find in my mailbag.

Soon after I started middle school I was an expert on a bicycle, and I could manoeuvre the route to school: the streets were narrow and buses were wide and horse-drawn flatbeds were slow, and sometimes men would catch up and ride next to you, whispering lewd messages into your ear. But, all things considered, life was spectacularly good: upon entering middle school I was chosen to be a librarian's assistant. I had not set foot in a library until then, and two roomfuls of books on tall shelves almost promised the happily-ever-after. Twice a week another student assistant and I stayed until five thirty, giving out books through a window to the many hands who fought to give us paper slips with Dewey numbers written on them (each student was allowed to put down five numbers at a time and was allowed to check out one book). After closing, we shelved the books, cleaned out the slips left on the floor, and then were allowed our privilege: we could check out two books.

Within a few months, I had finished all the books on the literature shelves (the 800s, as I began to think of them). They were of uneven quality, good only for the undiscriminating palate of a hungry mind. But the fact that one could have access to so many books—that was enough to celebrate about growing up.

The only trouble I had with my middle school education then was English. A majority of my classmates came from a cluster of government and military agencies nearby: the Chinese Military Academy, the headquarters of Military Intelligence, the Ministry of National Security and an army hospital. Children like me, who came from a more civilian and common background, would have a hard time understanding their upbringing: having household staff; parents travelling abroad on journalistic missions (spies, really, I was told); buses to deliver them to school and pick them up after; free English lessons long before they had entered middle school. The first week of middle school I cried every night: I couldn't memorize half of the ABC song, I had trouble telling the difference between "I" and "l", and if words shared common letters and appeared in the same lesson I became hopelessly confused. Words that tripped me in each other's disguise: ruler and rubber; pain and gain ("no pain, no gain"); four and five; ear and year.

You need an English–Chinese dictionary, the librarian—seeing that I tried to write out every English lesson ten times every day—told me. I didn't even know there was something called an English–Chinese dictionary. My only access to English then was in our textbook, which, other than letters and words, had sentences like "Long live the Chinese Communist Party" and "A friend in need is a friend indeed".

Where does one find a dictionary, I asked her, and she told me about this bookshop called the Foreign Language Bookshop. Her directions were so detailed and precise that I had little trouble finding the place: near a railway junction, in an alley, behind a food market, and flanked by a shoe-repair stall and a stand selling fresh tofu. All librarians, I sometimes think, are fairy godmothers in disguise.

The entrance to the bookshop, not wider than our apartment door, led to a narrow and long space. There were shelves of dictionaries and textbooks—English, German, French, Japanese, Russian, Spanish, Italian, and some others. It was the first bookshop that I walked into, and I was overwhelmed and overjoyed that here, as in the library, I could take any book I wanted off a shelf. There were books published by the Foreign Language Press, and they all had oil paintings as covers, which was foreign to me. *A Tale of Two Cities*, *The Mill on the Floss*, *The Woman in White*, *Uncle Tom's Cabin*, *The Adventures of Tom Sawyer*—these were the few books I remember, their Chinese titles printed on the cover too. I opened a book randomly; the text was entirely in English. I understood why my grandmother called her husband "bright-eyed and unseeing"—this must be how my illiterate grandfather felt when he saw any written words. However, I did recognize all the "I"s standing alone, while an "l" never appeared by itself. Even that encouraged me. Imagine: some day I'd be able to read these words and sentences!

At the end of the shelves there was an entrance into a second room, with a heavy cotton curtain separating the two sections of the bookshop. Next to the curtain, written in many languages, was a warning: Foreign Visitors Not Allowed.

If you knew (and know) China as I've known it, you would see the oddity and humour in that sign. When we grew up we called all foreigners "international friends", and to make them feel welcome and special was a political priority. In college, my best friend, when courted by a Korean student whom she did not want to see, was chased down the hallway by the dorm auntie; "an international friend" was waiting at the building entrance, she told my friend, and her refusal to meet the man would leave an unseemly "international reflection" on our school. Chances are, if you are a foreigner in China you are as close to royalty as you will ever be (unless you are a genuine prince or princess); it's still a land of fairy tales if you know where to look.

In any case, a place that did not allow foreigners to enter was one I must see, and enter I did. Curiouser and curiouser! The room beyond the curtain, a square not much bigger than the bedroom my sister and I shared with our grandfather, was full of books that didn't look like books. There were no shelves, and everything sat in high piles. One had to pick one's way carefully to avoid causing an avalanche. A man sitting at a desk by the entrance looked at me and returned to his paperwork. There were not many people in this room, and I must not have looked like someone who could afford or understand the treasures in this room.

In fact, the man was right. I could barely afford an English–Chinese dictionary in the other room. I did not have an allowance, though I had lunch money, and I already knew that I could scrimp and get enough money for a dictionary in a week. But what about this roomful of non-books? They were all photocopied materials, bound crudely, with light blue paper as cover. There was not even a Chinese title to tell me what they were. Oh the world was so close yet so far away, separated from mine by a language I had yet to master.

(Though the bookshop manager had foreseen the necessity to bar international friends, copyright was a completely unknown concept to most people at the time. Piracy—from bookshops to the internet—is a complicated issue in China. In my own case, I owe much of my education to pirated books, yet I'm also aware that, despite having refused to have my work translated into Chinese, people do so with impunity and publish translations both online and in print magazines without any communication with me.)

Once, after I had won a literary award, a journalist asked me if I had had a celebratory dinner. One of my many vices, I told him, was that I don't like food. Lucky you, he said, but then you don't know what you've missed.

I laughed, though my thought at that moment was: you don't know what I didn't miss. I spent three years of middle school eating noodles for lunch—twenty-one cents a meal for soupy noodles with a ladle of soy sauce on top. (By way of comparison, here were my other options: for rice and a vegetable dish it was forty cents; rice with a meat dish fifty cents; dumplings sixty; a platter of paper-thin cold cuts—no more than eight pieces—ten cents; an ice-cream bar twelve cents.) I can barely touch noodles now; I can eat cereal all day long. I must have destroyed my palate in middle school as I destroyed my eyes in third grade. But all, one must say, for a good cause!

And the money I saved: I've never felt so rich as I felt in middle school. And I've never splurged as I did then. Before long I owned two English–Chinese dictionaries, which I read voraciously; I also owned almost all the available English textbooks—textbooks not for middle school or high school but university students. One of them started with an article (touristy, in retrospect) about Cambridge University; another a Dylan Thomas essay (I didn't know who this person was but liked the essay); another a reportage about D-Day (which I had yet to learn about in world history).

Before long I started to covet the books in the inner section of the bookshop. Yes, an ugly duckling has to become a swan.

This is, of course, a story with a happy ending. And so rarely does a story have such a happy ending. Within a couple of years I'd gained enough confidence in my English (and found more ingenious ways to scrimp) that I started to become a regular customer in the inner section of the bookshop. Those piles on the floor were not books, but the *Reader's Digest*, photocopied, four issues bound together into a volume. They were costly, but they were entirely in English, and they were kept secret from most people, and they were my treasures. Down the rabbit hole I plunged. To this day I believe I've read more issues of *Reader's Digest* than anyone I've met; and more thoroughly, no doubt, as I paid close attention to every ad, every insert, every illustration (badly reproduced photos especially). The annotations I made in those volumes were as comprehensive as those I have made in *War and Peace* or Chekhov's stories in later life.

The bookshop is long gone, demolished along with the marketplace and the shoe-repair shop and the old Beijing. But never, I can say with certainty, has there been a bookshop that has provided so much magic in my life. There a girl found her prince in the pirated copies of *Reader's Digest*. An unworthy match? No, not at all. All that offers a happy ending is a good fairy tale.

If You Wound a Snake…

ALAA AL ASWANY

In 2011 my book *Egypt on the Reserve Bench* was published. It was a collection of articles in which I tried to explain how Egypt's potential was in a state of complete paralysis due to the dictatorship. I was invited to book signings in a number of bookshops. Book signings are both useful and enjoyable. An author usually writes for a public who cannot see him, and whenever an author listens to his readers he learns new things which can be of use to him in his writing.

On 23rd January I went to a book signing in the Dar El Shorouk bookshop in Mohandeseen—a bookshop as large, well-stocked and as grand as any big bookshop in London or New York. Mohandeseen is a middle-class district in which most Cairenes would aspire to live, and at the signing I expected to see readers from Mohandeseen: well-groomed men in designer casual and society ladies wearing the latest fashions, all peppering their conversation with English; people who generally derived enjoyment from culture and refinement; people who resented corruption and oppression in theory as they were much less exposed to them than the masses; people who favoured gradual political reform because they feared that any violent or fundamental change might deprive them of the *dolce vita* they were blessed with. That was the type of readership I was expecting, but the moment I stepped inside the crowded bookshop I was surprised by a different scene. The readers were much more varied. There were young and old, middle-class as well as poor people whose appearance might have seemed out of place in this upmarket shop. The crowd was so large that the management had had to open up two more rooms, each equipped with a screen so that everyone could follow the discussion.

In those days, Egypt was seething with anger as the elections had been grotesquely rigged so that Mubarak's party gained an absolute majority. The constitution had been amended specifically so that the president's son, Gamal Mubarak, could inherit power. Police oppression had increased to the point where any Egyptian could be tortured for the slightest reason. It was common knowledge that the police were above the law and that they could even get away with killing innocent citizens. All over social media there was mobile footage showing the police meting out gruesome torture to Egyptians. A few weeks earlier, the police in Alexandria had killed a young man called Khaled Said in an act of revenge for him having uploaded a video showing police officers divvying up hashish from a drug bust. The photograph of Khaled Said's mangled face, the complicity of the authorities in the investigation and their attempts to exculpate the killers all led to a surge in anger from the youth of the country. A Facebook page, "We are all Khaled Said", was created with hundreds of thousands joining it in the very first hours. The page called upon Egyptians to join in the demonstration on 25th January, which was also "Police Day" in Egypt. The message would be to object to police brutality against Egyptians and to demand a change in Egypt's political system. The fall and flight of the Tunisian dictator Ben Ali had shown the Egyptian people that a revolution could put an end to tyranny.

It was against this background that the book signing was being held, just two days before the anti-Mubarak demonstration. The atmosphere in the bookshop felt different from other book signings. It felt like a student gathering or a workers' sit-in. Everyone seemed strangely agitated, as if they wanted to express something or other, to state publicly what they were thinking or to declare something for the record. I said a few words about the subject matter of the book and the need for regime change and then I opened up the floor for discussion. Usually, whenever I hold a seminar, a state security agent comes to stir up trouble or to be so provocative that the discussion turns into a shouting match.

The first person to speak was a young woman in her twenties. With an edge of aggression to her voice she told me:

"I don't understand the secret of your hostility towards Mubarak. He is a democratic president, but circumstances have compelled him to institute democracy a step at a time. Egypt isn't Switzerland and the ordinary Egyptian can't handle democracy. When all is said and done, you just write books but President Mubarak bears responsibility for eighty-five million people. There may be some beauty in what you write, but it's a pack of lies and I don't believe a word of it."

I decided not to rise to the provocation. I answered calmly:

"You have every right not to believe what I write but my works have been translated into thirty-five languages and I am proud to have millions of readers who do. You are wrong to say that I am *just* a writer, because writing is a profession of the utmost difficulty. If you've read some Egyptian history, you'll be aware that Egyptians have been fighting for democracy since the nineteenth century. The meaning of democracy is justice, and not only every human but every creature needs justice. Personally I don't know Mubarak well enough to like or dislike him, but he's the dictator responsible for the corruption, brutality and poverty Egyptians have been suffering from. As for you saying that Mubarak is democratic, I have never heard of a democratic president who ruled his country for thirty years non-stop."

There was enthusiastic applause but an argument soon broke out between the young woman who had just spoken and other women sitting near her who accused her of being a state security plant. Voices called out for her to be ejected from the bookshop. I managed to convince them to let her be (although she soon made her own way out of the shop). The discussion resumed and I soon noticed that people's views seemed to correlate to their age group. The older readers spoke about change with a sort of despair, saying that what had taken place in Tunisia couldn't possibly happen in Egypt because the regime here was too strong and well-established and had powerful tools of oppression. The young people, on the other hand, asked me whether I was going to take part in the demonstrations on 25th January. To that I responded:

"I'm going to take part in the demonstrations and I call upon all those who want change to come out on 25th January. If we turn out in great numbers we'll be able to change this country."

There was a murmur of satisfaction from the young people and then a chic elderly lady raised her hand and asked me:

"Do you believe that change will come about in Egypt?"

"Absolutely. And it will come about sooner than we think," I replied.

The old lady smiled as if trying to conceal her sarcasm:

"And do you think you could explain the reasons for your optimism?"

"I'm a novelist," I said. "And I always strive to understand people. Egyptians can no longer put up with what's happening."

A young woman stood up and said:

"I'm a student at the College of Engineering at Cairo University and I want to say something to you all: my uncle is a police officer and he gave me a dire warning not to go out on 25th January. He told me in no uncertain terms that the police have received clear instructions to open fire on demonstrators."

There was tense silence. Then I asked her:

"And what are you going to do?"

Without a second thought she answered:

"I'm most definitely going to take part in the demonstrations. I could never forgive myself if I let my colleagues down."

Applause echoed throughout the bookshop and then I said:

"Now you see why I am an optimist. Courageous young people like that will not allow themselves to be defeated."

The evening ended with the book signing and the readers taking selfies of themselves with me. The next day the press coverage of the event was completely skewed, with one newspaper claiming that I had warned the young people against demonstrating, telling them that I would not be coming out on 25th January. Another newspaper reported that the audience had attacked me and rejected what I wrote on the grounds that I was trying to bring down the state and stir up pandemonium. Those false reports did not really worry me because I have grown used to them and because I know that the Egyptian readership does not generally have much faith in the media as it is all under the control of the state security police. Despite my enthusiasm for the 25th January demonstrations and my appeal to the young people to take part in them, I kept my expectations low to avoid being stricken by a sense of frustration. At that time I was still working on my novel *The Automobile Club of Egypt* and I woke up early in the morning as usual, worked on until noon, had some lunch, took a nap and then in the early evening I went out to Tahrir Square where I found a huge number of demonstrators. Young people kept shaking my hand and one said:

"Do you remember me? I was at your book signing in the shop in Mohandeseen the day before yesterday. We were a group of students and we hadn't been able to make up our minds. But after your encouragement, we all decided to come out today."

At that moment, there were at least twenty thousand of us in Tahrir Square, all shouting against the dictator. Happy as I felt, I did not let my optimism carry me away because we had been kettled in by thousands of state security police and scores of armoured cars. They could crush us at any moment. At about 8 p.m. an enormous demonstration reached the square, having started out in Nahiyya, a working-class district of Cairo. Those demonstrators set upon the security police concertedly and with gusto, and succeeded in breaking through the police lines into the square. There were now around fifty thousand demonstrators in the square and the security police were still waiting for their orders. There was a festive mood and a fellow demonstrator turned and said to me:

"At last we've managed to mobilize people against tyranny. Today is the start of change."

At twenty to one in the morning the gates of hell opened. The armoured cars fired off a salvo of tear gas grenades from all directions, and the gas lay so thick in the air that scores of people fainted, including some of the policemen who were firing the gas at us. As demonstrators started rushing to try and get out of the square they were set upon by plainclothes policemen who hustled them into police vans. The plan was obviously to leave demonstrators the choice of choking on the tear gas or being arrested as they tried to flee. I was lucky in being able to escape into a small side street where there were no policemen, and I kept running until I reached the other side of the downtown district. I found myself standing in front of Cinema Metro with about twenty young demonstrators who, like me, had managed to get out of the square without being arrested. It was now past one in the morning. The street was empty, but suddenly an old street sweeper passed by, dragging a long, worn-out broom. It was an odd sight to see, but it was even odder when he shouted out gruffly:

"If you wound a snake, you have to finish him off. Kill the snake before he does you in."

The young demonstrators hailed the sweeper who trundled off with his broom like the hero in a Greek tragedy.

"So what do you think?" one of the demonstrators asked me in a friendly tone. "What should we do now?"

"I'm glad the demonstration succeeded," I said. "That is the strongest message against the dictator. Let's be happy with what we've achieved today. I think we should go home for now and demonstrate again tomorrow."

"Won't happen!" I was surprised to hear one of the demonstrators say. "Won't happen. We're not going home now."

"Do you think you'll be able to arrest Mubarak tonight?" I asked. "Our struggle demands that we be patient."

They started arguing with me and I looked at them and realized for the first time that I didn't understand them. Another of the young guys came over to me and told me emphatically:

"Listen, mister. I'm from Ismailiya. I got my science baccalaureate five years ago and I'm still unemployed. I've got nothing. No work here, no chance of getting work in another country, and no hope of being able to get married. I have come to Cairo to get rid of Mubarak or die. I'm already dying. Just imagine that I…"

His words dried up and he burst into tears. I took a few steps so I was right in front of the group of young people and asked them bluntly:

"And what is it that you want?"

Almost as one they replied: "We're going back to the square!"

I went back to the square with them, where we were gradually joined by groups of demonstrators who, like us, had fled from the tear gas and, like us, had then decided to make their way back to the square. That is how I witnessed the start of the revolution.

Translated from the Arabic by Russell Harris

Desiderium:
The Accidental
Bookshop of Nairobi

YVONNE ADHIAMBO OWUOR

We met, sometimes, mother and I, within timeless words dreamed by others. We played tag in worlds inhabited by letter-created djinns, and phantoms and elves and hobbits too. A child, a daughter among many, craving the many ways a mother, also a teacher, expresses her "I love yous". We met in variegated worlds made from the words of so many authors: the Brothers Grimm, Hans Christian Andersen, Marjorie Oludhe Macgoye, Enid Blyton, Grace Ogot, J.R.R. Tolkien, James Herriot, Wilbur Smith, Jack London, Roald Dahl, C.S. Lewis, L.M. Montgomery. These peddled worlds inside worlds, within which Nairobi, the city, Kileleshwa, the suburb, could be subsumed by orcs, ogres, talking trees, Noddy and boy and girl sleuths. Mother brought home these books once a month. They came wrapped in brown packages and were stamped "Westlands Sundries".

*　　*　　*

One day, mother escorted my younger sister and me into the timeless realm from which storybooks came. We dressed up. We had to be "suitably attired" to enter such a magical place. This dressing up was as the click-click of Dorothy's *Wizard of Oz* red slippers.

The bookshop was a long illuminated rectangle.

Choose one, mother said.

Budgets were more tightly defined in those days.

Choose one.

Only one?

We touched the spines of books, sniffed pages for the new book scents—each so different. We were in paradise because there was no (offending) school textbook in sight to destroy our illusions! There were toys and puzzles and some stationery, but no school mathematics or geography texts or workbooks. Enid Blyton was there, the perennial queen. Magazines that other children would swarm around, but not us.

We saw Tolkien and C.S. Lewis and Hans Christian Andersen. The politics of race, identity, culture and "appropriate-for" had not yet penetrated our imaginations. For us, it was plausible that Janet and John would go tobogganing down winter slopes and evoke in us a yearning for winter in a city that promised to be Arcadian (though it now looks less idyllic). It was not yet the time to understand that the gollywog in Noddy was a problematic presence. To go into the bookshop was to enter a boundary-less territory where anything could be experienced. A hundred Enid Blytons, fifty Wilbur Smiths, Carolyn Keene's Nancy Drew, Franklin Dixon's Hardy Boys and Jack London, whose works made us cry and yearn for more winters. It would take a long time to learn to separate the world we lived in from the ones we travelled through in words.

Choose one.

Only one?

My sister and I tiptoed in nervous reverence before the bounty of titles, touching book spines, peeping at the "big people's" books on our way to the children's section. At the children's books shelves, we would discover *Anne of Green Gables*. We chose her. We took her home. She became one of us. We would fight over her, learn to daydream as she did, and wait for Gilbert Blythe to pass by. Later the book would be covered with plastic, and become a tradable commodity and currency among school friends. The barter created access to other storybooks, companions to be sought after, bargained with, and mourned when lost. Mother would review the books we chose. We followed her to the counter where the book people presided over the shop. From a child's height they looked so alien—a greying man, his dark-haired daughter. I was jealous of the book people and the country of literature they could access at will. Nairobi's frontiers were boundless inside the shop; they contained, for example, Tolkien's Middle Earth.

It is 9.30 a.m. on Wednesday, 6th April 2016. I return to the original site of the bookshop of my childhood. But this is Nairobi in the twenty-first century. It is in a delirium of reconstructive surgery. Cosy shops have been replaced by glossy gleaming surfaces that exalt gadgets. Westlands Sundries in the Westlands district appears to have relocated. The area of the old shop is taken over by a bland and steel sameness that is wounding this city, spaces of memory buried in rubble without sentiment. The brushing past of phantoms of loss. Within me, a twinge of grief. I leave, aiming for the bookshop's sister outlets, including the iconic Nation Bookshop, in the middle of the central business district…

… gone.

Surprise. The small familiar touchstones of life do crumble into nothing. I can recall that as a child who collected words, I found one in a story from middle England:

Fugacious.

I had sought its meaning from my father since my school dictionary did not contain it. Daddy was a wordsmith. He explained it. *Ephemeral. Evanescent.* Does not last. Like fog. *Fugacious.* Nobody ever thinks of sending the children of a particular memory-scape a notice of change of use so they can try to retrieve the portions of themselves—in my case, shadowy shards stored within books on familiar bookshelves.

It is official. I have become part of that generation that stares at fresh spots in old landscapes and mutters, "When I was young there used to be…" I have grown older. My city has grown younger, cosmetically adjusting its face with no nostalgia for its (in our eyes, always) beautiful past or care for the feelings of those it had previously sheltered differently.

I gape at the gap where the bookshop used to be, as if time might fall away and reveal the past intact. An elderly watchman dressed in faded blue with red stripes crosses the street and stops next to me. Later, I will remember that, without seeing the irony, we had stood beside one of Nairobi's roadside booksellers from whom one could obtain a copy of the *Odyssey*, Petina Gappah's *Book of Memory* and last month's *Vanity Fair* magazine for the price of a new self-help-change-your-thoughts book from one of the mall bookshops.

"Where did the old bookshop go?" I murmur to the watchman.

He says, "Walihama." They moved. We stare at the spot in the wall. "Many stop here," he observes, "and ask the same question."

Silence. This had been a locale of my slow coming of age. This was the place to find the literature of becoming woman, being woman, yearning, failing, falling in love, falling out of love, seeking, desiring, losing, finding the world, losing the soul, travelling, returning, coming home, leaving home and giving meaning to life. This bookshop, and its familiar tentacles, was always there: a sentinel, guardian and guiding rod. Behind us, the hooting, screeches, chatter and other noises of life going on. I comfort myself. "They have moved" is better than "They have disappeared".

*   *   *

The late season Nairobi rains are furious. Dammed streams have turned into almost forgotten rivers that rush across brand new roads, making a mockery of "national vision" plans that are intended to lead Kenya into a glossy, honeyed Canaan. Driving—or, more accurately, boating—beyond the city limits, catching a glimpse of streams where long ago as children we fished for tadpoles and golden fish, which we ferried away in clear bottles. They never did survive. Crossing to the "other side" of town into Gigiri.

The Village Market is a sprawling red-roofed white-brick mall with water features, a haphazard collection of units that somehow work: pretty stalls, shops and food courts. Nairobi's beautiful people mingle with those of the nations of the world who are here for lunch—the United Nations offices and various embassies are close by.

Meandering down the mall's numerous corridors that lead off to glamorous shops touting the world's shiny bounty, I stumble upon my destination. I had walked into a softly lit bookshop to ask directions of a bespectacled woman at the counter. "Hello. Could you help me? Where is Westlands Sundries?"

"You are here."

"What?"

"Indeed."

In cursive script, on the wall above the till, an impressive legend: "*Between the Lines*".

*   *   *

"Here" is a capacious rectangle built on two levels. Gone is the aesthetic of a single space differentiated only by shelves and book categories. There are compartments here. One for comics and graphic novels, another for children's literature, others for the bodice-rippers we used to giggle over and sneak glimpses at—everything so organized and defined. Looking around, like an archaeologist might, I sought relics of the past beyond the veneer of the new. Plenty of children's books, including the ones that were anathema in my day. The "Africana" that had made the bookshop famous had a corner of their own, as did cookbooks from all parts of the world. There was a book on Celtic aesthetics, a section on personal and spiritual empowerment, and another for biographies. A section labelled "General Ignorance" is filled with adult puzzle books, and profound knowledge succinctly packed—*What Is a Supernova?* Vestiges remain of the haphazard loveliness of random placements—thankfully (for me) not all books are alphabetically arranged, so in places a book lover can indulge the art of sensing one's path to desired words and worlds, or call up a guide to point the way. The Penguin series are there: orange, blacks and whites, and now with a strip of colour. In my childhood, these were like a future promise made up of impossible names: Sartre, Eliot, Nabokov and Dostoevsky. These are no longer strangers.

In a niche on the ground level, maps and travel books summon up the past. Wilfred Thesiger is still here; old names, old friends; traces of permanence. It is unfortunate that Paul Theroux and his incessant anti-Africa whining is positioned so close to Thesiger. Other books on the shelves recall a season when it was easier to idolize my country; it has since fallen off its pedestal. The section that Heinemann's African Writers' Series used to occupy is tenanted by a fresh wave of writers writing Africa: Selasi, Mengiste, Lalami, Baingana, Adichie, Cole, Wainaina, Ontita, Mda, Wrong and Gurnah among others. The covers of these books are a stunning mosaic of a complex African imaginary.

I look around. Not even the dust of old dreams persists. No Enid Blytons, no Wilbur Smiths, no Hardy Boys, Nancy Drew or Famous Fives. The Norse, Greek, Roman and other gods are confined to a new twilight. Portions of their lives reside in comic books—portions they would not recognize as themselves.

Touching the shelves, my nose close to the spines of books, I find books that breep, squeak and, *the horror*, presume to talk back. I meet old friends in new shapes: *Charlotte's Web*, *The Lion, the Witch and the Wardrobe*, and I tell Dr Seuss, "I remember you." There are new creatures in old places: long-toothed Gruffalo, *Diary of a Wimpy Kid*, *Diary of a Worm*, J.K. Rowling's Harry Potter in its assorted manifestations; *The Hunger Games*, *Girl Online*, *Dork Diaries*, the *Divergent* series, *Horrid Henry*s and *The World of Norm*. I have fallen forward and emerged into a new realm of words!

*　　*　　*

I head downstairs to introduce myself to the woman at the till. Her name is Elizabeth Kitema. I explain how I went looking for them, how long it took to find them. I realize my tone sounds aggrieved. I pull myself together. "Why did you leave Westlands?"

She watches me for a second before answering carefully. "The ownership of the building changed. We had to leave." Something in her face suggests that this is a no-go area. So we talk some more about books, life and the meaning of book-vending. Nostalgia's bug is catching. Elizabeth has been with the bookshop since 1977 when Yasmin Manji, only child of its founder, bibliophile Sayed Mohamed, took it over. "I went through the doors as a nervous little girl. I grew up as a woman among these books that have fed my family," Elizabeth says.

"I must have seen you," I say.

"Nation Bookshop?"

I nod. Nation Bookshop was often mentioned in travel guides and had been a staple of Kenya's tourist circuit. Elizabeth continues, her gaze turning inwards to the persistent past. "You remember we were a major tourist stop? For Kenyans too. But travellers identified most with us. Visitors could find the books of Africa and Kenya that were difficult to find anywhere else."

It is true, for Sayed Mohamed would travel the country and the world hunting for out-of-print Kenyan and African books, which he would then arrange to have reprinted and republished under the Westlands Sundries imprint.

Our family copy of *The Lunatic Express*, the story of a railway line that forged a country, belongs to this category. Mr Mohamed also collaborated with the late documentarian and photographer Mohammed Amin on a couple of volumes that he published and sold at the bookshop.

Elizabeth also remembers how many people would return to the bookshop armed with new stories about their lives. More anecdotes of human encounters mediated by a bookshop: the Japanese tourists brought in by a diligent master tour guide, a Kenyan bibliophile married to a Japanese woman, who would give impromptu book reviews and lectures in Japanese to his clients in the shop before tailoring book choices for them, based on what he thought they ought to learn.

"Maps," pipes up a medium-height man, with the kind of rough-edged face that evokes weathered male beauty in black and white photographs. Deep eyes, the kind that listen so that he does not need to say much. He had been eavesdropping. This was Jackson Mutuku. He has worked all his life in bookshops. He joins in. "Those tourists would leave with maps of different parts of Kenya." A soft smile. "He loved maps. He read them as books. He is dead now." His voice is tinged with odd regret as he continues: "The city was filled with visitors then. It truly belonged to the world. Our shop was always full of people."

Silence.

We stand around the till, lost in the memory of a past which feels, in that moment, so much more intense, simple and human. A woman enters with her baby daughter. She heads straight to the children's section and sits the child on the warm, carpeted and colourful ground. You get the sense that she just needed to breathe differently, to pause a while before she continued with her tasks for the day. Ten minutes later, the baby is asleep. The woman leaves without buying anything, without saying anything. Elizabeth and Jackson are unfazed. "Book people," smiles Jackson. "We know them. They come into a bookshop to find themselves. Book people."

A bulked-up man limps in. He is looking for a book on fixing motorbikes. Jackson goes off to locate something for him. He browses through the selection. He talks about rolling on his bike. How it fell on him. He glances at a page. He chooses one book. He leaves. I ask about that, the notion of bookshop as a mini confessional where one deposits revelations of one's true self. Both Elizabeth and Jackson laugh.

In essence, they tell me, a bookshop is a crucible of human habit. The character of a person—their loves, loathings, hopes and fears—can be discerned in the books they choose, their movement in and about the bookshop, and in their interactions with literature and also their book vendor. They imagine that the habits of clients also help form and inform the character of the bookseller. "We depend on their patronage. Whatever they demand, we must listen and attend to it, no matter the manner in which the request is made."

They have had a glimpse into the many modes of human beingness. In the morning, a woman can come in and show them her ring while singing, "Do you have a book on wedding planning?" In the afternoon, another will stop by to whisper, "Can you recommend a book on managing grief? I lost my son last week."

A bookshop memory: a businessman in a dark suit struggling to keep his composure rushes in desperately seeking a "how-to" business book. *Not this one. Do you have another one?* he pleads and then he breaks down. "I mortgaged the family home for a business loan. My wife and children do not know. *They* are coming to auction everything tomorrow. There is nothing left."

"What do you do?" I finally ask.

Jackson answers. "We listen. We look for the books. If they want to, they buy. But we also know that sometimes people just need to pour out their hearts to another human being." Jackson shrugs. "It costs nothing to say sorry."

Right then, a stately woman strolls in. She is a traveller. From her greeting and accent, she is probably North American. She wanders through the shop and returns to the till with six children's books. She says she is buying these for a book vendor she ran into in one of Kenya's more distant counties. She says the vendor's nomad client needed puzzle books for his children. This is her second sally into the bookshop. She had stopped there when she first landed in Kenya two months ago.

Two teenagers talk to each other while their phones

erupt with zany sounds. They head straight to the graphic novels section. Their rapid exchange is about Jon Snow and *Game of Thrones*, interspersed with the expression "Rad!" I watch them surreptitiously. In the manner of old-timers, I recall how impossible it would have been for my generation to walk into a place without acknowledging the adults. We would not have dared broadcast our personal business at the top of our voice in a *bookshop*!

Elizabeth glances quickly at the pair and returns to our conversation. She says that she feels that the quality of people's love for books has changed over the years. It is an interesting idea. Jackson agrees. He worries that new technologies are fragmenting the attention span of young people.

I ask the unavoidable question: "Is there a future for books and bookshops as they are now?"

Elizabeth and Jackson merely offer wry smiles.

Around us flutters a ghostly impression of the ephemeral.

Later, Elizabeth reaches for her phone. "You have to speak to Yasmin," she says.

A woman with a laugh in her voice says "Hello".

"Is this the book lady?" I ask.

Yasmin giggles.

Later she asks, "Do you know that ours was the first real bookshop in Nairobi?"

*   *   *

The vision started in the time before 1971, the year that Westlands Sundries became a legal entity. It is the story of a man's profound love affair with books in an era when television broadcasts stopped at 10 p.m. and there was plenty of time to read and talk. Sayed Mohamed, in between his accounting duties, would lurk in auction houses waiting to bid on book lots. The books were for his own consumption. He had already acquired a large collection when a friend who had built an office block in Westlands asked if he wanted a shop space downstairs. He took the space and registered the business as "Westlands Sundries", intending to sell anything—toys, stationery, household goods—not yet imagining that the books he also sold would become the mainstay.

Yasmin, his daughter, would visit the shop with her father before she went to school, and attended to it after school. She saw the books take over the store.

"It was inevitable," Yasmin notes, "for literature was my father's true passion. Anyone who walked into the shop to buy an oven, more often than not, ended up leaving with a book or two."

We laugh.

I met with Yasmin a few days later. Though deeply modest about her spectacular achievements in the service of literature in Kenya, she acknowledges that my honorific—"book lady"—is not uncommon. So many children journeyed into life and adulthood by way of this enterprise that co-opted her whole family. Yasmin is a woman through whom life shines in colour, hope and joy. Ageless and gorgeous, her hair is glossy black; her clothes, lilac and gold and green, reflect her warm spirit. Yasmin has a detailed recall of faces, of family book-shopping routines; a memory of the children who showed up every weekend with their parents to buy "one book each", others who turned up on week-days after school, still others who bought books in bulk before the school holidays, the children living in faraway corners of Kenya who travelled twice a year to the shop to stock up on storybooks, the children who skipped school to hide out in the shop and read. She has a memory of the adults too—numerous clients who turned up with stories of their lives, who stopped by because they were lonely, the ones who showed up twice a week as a matter of routine to buy a book, any book. Since this is a journey linked to nostalgia and childhood, we stay with the memory of the children, one of whom, Christina Leone, by coincidence, strolls in and plonks herself down on a chair to join our interview session.

Double coincidence. It turns out that Christina and I had gone to the same convent school—she was a few years older. She was the swimming captain, one of the lofty "big girls". Christina and Yasmin became friends after Yasmin got weary of chasing her away from the bookshop, where Christina would show up often to figure out puzzles, play with model aeroplanes and miniature animals, read story-books and decline to leave. They share a loud laugh over that memory before we return to the topic of Westlands Sundries.

Yasmin took over the bookshop in 1977. "This was my fate and destiny," she says. "I did not know anything else. I always knew that the shape of my life would be built around the bookshop."

I attempt to broach the topic of their leaving the fifty-year flagship store in Westlands. A grimace temporarily mars Yasmin's serene features. This is a sore point. I abandon the topic. One day I will return to it. Not today. In our general conversation, one senses the trauma of this probably unexpected amputation from the site of a girl's moulding as daughter, businesswoman, wife, mother, citizen and bibliophile.

We return to the theme of books as we settle around a table in a café that proclaims "*Happiness is a cup of coffee and a good book.*" Yasmin says she holds her meetings here because it is designed for book lovers.

There are books stacked up on a shelf behind her.

"There is such pleasure in the smell of a book." She hesitates as if afraid of exaggerating. Quietly, she explains, "It is such a personal thing." She leans forward, "A book is not just a product; a book is an experience. To understand them you must have a feel for books." Her eyes sparkle.

Yasmin is a gentle raconteuse with a self-deprecating sense of humour, a large-hearted woman immersed in life and its ceaseless questions. She is a soul who has taken intense journeys in and through her bookshop: business journeys, human journeys, journeys into and through discovery and loss, mostly of cherished ones like her husband Noorudin Manji, who died in 2011 and had overseen the logistics of book retailing. She had understood then that she could not give in. She had to learn to do what he had been doing. There was a city and community that needed her to keep the bookshop open. "There was never a plan B for me," Yasmin reiterates.

This is why there is still a Westlands Sundries in a Nairobi where bookshops are a casualty of the illusion of progress. Her father, having discovered his purpose in the world of literature, was never distracted by other glittering business prospects. Yasmin inherited this single-minded focus. Our conversation wanders. It returns to the shop. She says, "Father's bulwark was my mother Gulshan. She was the constant. When father went on his sourcing trips and to book fairs, she stood guard. She never sought the light for herself. But she stayed at her post until she died two years ago."

Sayed's passion was a flame that drew in his whole family. It translated into a space where the people that ended up working there are those like Elizabeth and Jackson who are open to the mystery of the world of books, insightful people who know where to find book titles, who neither fuss nor glare if someone unwraps the plastic covering of books so as to turn the pages, who have settled into the service of literature with no intention of changing tack, no matter how seductive the other offers they receive.

I ask, "How much did you change the shop after your father's years?"

Christina cuts in. "Yasmin's passions, her diversity of interests, all of these translated into greater varieties and categories on the bookshelves; you can see these for yourself. She has names for the infinity of new-book smells. Best of all, when you lingered in the bookshop, you got fed!"

Laughter.

As if on cue, Yasmin's two sons Zain and Zahid appear. Zain is intense, with dark marks under his eyes. By his own admission, he is a night owl; the morning causes him to growl. The taller son Zahid is watchful and quiet. He listens. He has a wicked sense of humour. The brothers tease one another and their mother constantly. Theirs is a relationship threaded with play. Yasmin is relinquishing control of the bookshop to them, a third generation taking over. They are curious about this interview. The brothers speak of growing up deluged by books in all available spaces, in every room. They joke that when they moved house it was because the books needed a bigger place to occupy.

Zain, who is the elder, remembers with a sense of irony "I never had to buy books. Made it difficult going into a bookshop abroad. What a struggle: the choice between reading the book now, or waiting to return home to Kenya where I could get it free." Zain's vision for Westlands Sundries is much in keeping with the trends of the present age: the graphic novels section is his innovation. The category has its followers. It is the space where the city's closet graphic novelists show up to find each other. The shop sells and promotes the posters and comics of some of Kenya's best, the only bookshop that does so in Nairobi. Today Zahid, diplomat in the making, oversees some of the bookshop's back-room stuff: stock control, bookkeeping, systems, licences. Zain, non-practising biochemist, is preparing for a Saturday free comic book day at the bookshop. Speciality events, niche marketing, author readings, gatherings of readers, multimedia—indicators of added dimensions to this bookshop's life? Yasmin listens to her sons with equanimity, glimpsing the future, as we do, in this discussion. She is serene about the inevitability of change, understanding that a resilient system absorbs shocks and reshapes itself to accommodate and grow from the opportunities presented by a new epoch. There are lessons here for my nostalgic self.

As we bring the interview to a close, Elizabeth turns up with a well-dressed man with round spectacles and an effusive manner. Yasmin rises to greet him with warmth. She then introduces us. His name is Eduardo Moreno—a UN worker, but also a photographer whose works have been widely published.

"We are talking about books," Yasmin says.

Eduardo notes that the bulk of his life has been spent reading books. We speak about the themes he explores in his photography. "Why did you choose Westlands Sundries to showcase your work, *Wooden Dreams*, in East Africa?" I ask.

He answers that it was not because they were the largest, slickest or most strategic, but it was because he felt that it was the place where books were most at home in Nairobi. "It is full of light so even I, with my eyes, can read the small print in books. It has life and space and energy. It is for people who are in love with books. They let me unwrap the plastic that covers books without rolling their eyes."

"Dust covers," Yasmin chips in. "We cover the books to protect them from dust discolouration."

Eduardo quips, "In other bookshops the plastic is a defence against readers. They forget that an important part of book buying comes from having a tactile connection with the pages." We laugh the laugh of those who "get" a secret code. As if in confidence, he adds, "Here you can stop. You can talk. You can walk through book worlds. You meet life. You make friends."

We leave the coffee shop in a chattering convoy.

For a moment, I forget that this is an interview. The spirit of the place has rid me of some unstated fear. With a fresh insight into its history, I feel secure in my memory of Westlands Sundries. *What endures?* I sometimes wonder. In this encounter, what endures are stories we are compelled to tell because of the people we have met and known in life and literature; what endures is the legacy of a man in love with books, who infused his wife and daughter, a city, a nation and the world with his passion. What endures are unexpected meetings that unfold in spaces warmed and touched by books.

Before I exit the bookshop, one more thing.

I explain.

"My mother, elegantly aged, and retired, keeps a garden she loves. In this season of Nairobi storms, her plants are suffering. Might you have a book on the management of waterlogged land?"

Jackson retrieves three possibilities. I choose one. At the till, Elizabeth slips it into a plain bag. No "Westlands Sundries" branding. However, I no longer need to be reminded that here I can reclaim a space where the sense of a constant "home" in a mercurial city abides.

Snow Day

MICHAEL DIRDA

On the morning of Friday, 22nd January 2016, Washington DC was preparing for snow. In fact, the city was hunkering down for a major blizzard. School had already been cancelled and the subway, astonishingly, would be closed all weekend. By that afternoon nothing would be moving across the white landscape except ploughs, salt trucks and people on cross-country skis.

Just the day before, my wife had fortuitously left for San Francisco and wouldn't be back until Tuesday. In other words, I was home alone, without any—what's the word I want?—supervision. After breakfast, a quick phone call confirmed that the Second Story Books warehouse, located in Rockville, Maryland, would stay open until the snow actually began to fall. According to the *Washington Post*'s weather gang, that wouldn't be until sometime after 1 p.m. Consequently, a resolute and determined bookman—especially one whose beloved spouse was on the other side of the country—might be able to paw through a half million books for perhaps three hours. Possibly even longer, if he was willing to risk driving home at the onset of the reputedly apocalyptic storm.

Thus at a little after 10 a.m. I was blithely making my way along Parklawn Drive through an area dominated by wholesale flooring outlets, self-storage companies and electrical and plumbing supply stores. While Second Story does maintain an open shop in Washington's bustling Dupont Circle, its offices and warehouse are out here in the suburban backwaters. Once upon a time, its owner, Allan Stypeck, operated additional Maryland outlets in Bethesda and Baltimore. But those days are long past. The used-book business has contracted significantly since the 1980s when the greater Washington metro area boasted forty or fifty shops.

They bore names like Book Alcove, Book Nook and Book Market, and many dealt principally in garage sale leftovers and current bestsellers, rather than antiquarian material. Still, the book-addled will glance around even the most lowly paperback exchange. After all, as the collector's mantra has it, anything can be anywhere. I remember unearthing Cyril Connolly's relatively scarce pamphlet *The Missing Diplomats*—published in England by the Queen Anne Press—in a junky magazine emporium near Union Station. It cost me a quarter, but finding this early account of the Burgess–Maclean spy case made my day since I was then a Connolly completist. On another Saturday, behind the counter of a Silver Spring shop not far from where I live now, I noticed a first in a fine jacket of Robert Penn Warren's *All the King's Men*. The dealer had priced it at $50, and soon after I bought the book—even then worth a thousand dollars—he realized his mistake.

Such discoveries keep collectors and scouts—as book runners are called in the US—coming back again and again. Once I picked up an inscribed copy of H.G. Wells's collected stories from a sidewalk cart marked "Any book, $4; six for $20". I stupidly crowed about this find in print and the shop's owner was properly miffed, but he drew lots of new customers as a result. Of course, such bargains are far harder to come by in the digital age, since sellers tend to hunch over their computers all day checking online prices at Abe or Amazon. Today, it's unlikely one could notice on an open shelf—as I once did in Winchester, Virginia, the birthplace of the immortal Patsy Cline—a first edition of Richard Garnett's *Twilight of the Gods*, inscribed by the author to his close friend, the painter Ford Madox Brown, and priced at a whopping $5.

Another example: when I first arrived in Washington in the late 1970s, I worked part time at an extremely downmarket bookshop on Sunday afternoons. Its owner would accept virtually any printed matter—even *Reader's Digest* Condensed Books—and in exchange offer some derisory amount in credit, never cash. But one Sunday Pat and Allen Ahearn—the owners of Quill & Brush, which specializes in fine modern firsts—charitably dropped off a couple of boxes of fiction they couldn't sell. Being tasked with shelving this better-than-usual stock, I noticed a novel written by a woman from my home town of Lorain, Ohio. Years later, I got Toni Morrison to sign that copy of *The Bluest Eye*. I just looked it up online to check its current value: at least $3,500.

While I have always admired tidy antiquarian bookshops, such places are usually too well curated for my taste. Sleepers are scarce. Bear in mind that I grew up the son of a working-class, shopaholic mother who loved bargains. If it wasn't marked down, usually by at least seventy-five per cent, she didn't give the item a second glance. With such a heritage, I naturally gravitate toward book barns and warehouses and thrift shops where the quantity of books takes precedence over any apparent quality. Yet in overwhelming abundance lies the possibility of overlooked treasure. For instance, from Second Story's warehouse I once scooped up a first of John Meade Falkner's *Moonfleet*—a thrilling Stevensonian adventure story—for a couple of bucks. Nowadays, the warehouse runs an almost continuous forty per cent off sale of its regular stock, while its huge bargain annexe charges $4 for a hardcover, sometimes less. On the morning of the gathering storm, the annexe hardcovers were going for $2 each.

I've never counted how many books I own, but my attic is stuffed with genre fiction from the late nineteenth and early twentieth century—needed for a big project—and the basement is solidly packed with recent novels and non-fiction, some of it on industrial shelving but the bulk in boxes piled higgledy-piggledy. It's really quite appalling. There's also a rented storage unit, which has sucked a fortune out of me, probably more than its contents are worth. If forced to guess, however, I'd estimate that I own between 15,000 and 20,000 books, conceivably more. From many quite reasonable points of view I have "too many books", but to my mind I just need more bookshelves. Or a bigger house.

Yet am I, in fact, a collector? Somewhere I read that if you couldn't lay your hands on any book you owned in five minutes, you were just an accumulator, a hoarder. I couldn't lay my hands on some of my books if I had five days to search for them. The great bibliographical scholar G. Thomas Tanselle contends that any true collection requires an overarching theme, a plan, defined limits. My only plan is to keep books I might need in my work or that I hope to read some day for my own sweet pleasure. That means Tarzan and the insidious Dr Fu Manchu as well as Dickens and Proust. The novelist and bookseller Larry McMurtry once observed that only those with basements or storage units like mine can enjoy the highly rarefied delight of scouting their own books: you never know what might be waiting at the bottom of the next box. Of course, McMurtry used to buy entire bookshops to stock the used and rare shelves of Archer City, Texas, his American version of Hay-on-Wye.

In my defence, I do suffer from an associative malady that permits me to justify acquiring almost any book. Take, at random, Leonard Merrick's *The House of Lynch*. Merrick is now an almost entirely forgotten writer, but he was once so popular that each volume in a standard set of his works was introduced by a celebrated contemporary, in the above case G. K. Chesterton. As it happens, I've collected Chesterton ever since I first read *The Man Who Was Thursday*, so it would make perfect sense to plunk down a dollar or two for Merrick's novel. In this case, though, I did manage to back away from the book. More clutter, I sternly said to myself. Of course, I now realize I should go back to that thrift store and see if *The House of Lynch* might still be there. After all, who but another Chesterton collector would want it?

The cement floor of the Second Story warehouse stands roughly three feet off the ground and there are loading bays for trucks on either side of the entrance. On that Friday morning, as Snowzilla was preparing to stomp Washington, I parked in an almost empty lot. Once inside, I said hello to Eddie, Second Story's most senior employee, who immediately started talking about the short-sightedness of any high school curriculum that didn't include *Kidnapped*. I grunted my assent, but couldn't really waste time on our usual chit-chat, given the approaching storm and many, many shelves to look through.

Still, I would argue that under most circumstances the conversation of used book dealers or obsessive collectors is the best conversation in the world. I remember once visiting Port Richmond Books, comparable in size to the Second Story warehouse, in a working-class suburb of Philadelphia. The owner's inner sanctum included a long library table, and around it that afternoon lounged a half-dozen locals, trading neighbourhood gossip and old war stories about Vietnam as they nibbled on cheese, pickles, good bread and Polish kielbasa. Nearby was a humming refrigerator filled with beer and soda, as well as a keg of Guinness. Greg Gillespie, the owner, handed me a glass and told me to help myself to the eats. Yes, I could take along my Guinness as I prowled through his miles of fiction. I was there for hours and bought a bunch of books and left half drunk. Best afternoon ever.

At the Second Story warehouse the "regular" stock is arranged in the usual sorts of categories—mysteries, biography, literary criticism—but there are unmarked sub-sections as well. On the tops of some random shelves loom sets of Thackeray, Carlyle and other eminent Victorians, while certain bookcases display specialty publications, such as the garish, faux rarities of the Easton Press, the austere volumes of the Library of America, and boxed titles from Heritage and the Folio Society. Occasionally, one sees little slips of paper protruding from between a book's pages; these slightly pricier titles are listed online. Second Story also sells graphics, movie posters, Asian art, vinyl records, VHS tapes, DVDs and CDs. Near the checkout is a table covered with cartons holding dilapidated issues of

Amazing, Weird Tales, Unknown, Thrilling Wonder Stories and other pulp magazines.

No matter how often I've gone to the warehouse I can never quite scout it all in one visit. Usually this is because of time pressure, often compounded with guilt that I should be writing or working in the garden or cooking dinner or simply doing something other than looking at old books. Over the years I've also learned the prudence of sneaking any newly acquired treasures into the house as covertly as possible. There's nothing like a baleful glare from one's beloved spouse to ruin a good day's booking, to use a word common among American collectors. Nowadays, though, I'm in top form only during my first four or five hours in a shop; after that my head starts to grow woozy and my eyes have trouble focusing. Yet I am nothing if not dogged. After all, during those few blissful hours my cares and worries are forgotten. As a boy, I could lose myself utterly in a book; now I seem to lose myself only in used bookstores. Alas, neither sweet surrender nor wide-eyed wonder, except fleetingly, is advisable for a professional reviewer. Moreover, I'm one who, even on holiday, can't start an Agatha Christie paperback without a pencil in his hand. My mind tends to interrogate any text, on the alert for clues, telling details, key passages, the secret engines of the story. As a result, while reading remains a pleasure, it's become a guarded pleasure, tinged with suspicion. Quite reliably, however, my heart still leaps with childlike joy at the sight of row after row of old books on shelves.

That particular Friday I first zoomed in on a couple of the bookcases where one finds slightly shabby titles from the nineteenth and early twentieth century. Straight off, I noticed an American first of Conan Doyle's *Adventures of Gerard*, priced on the flyleaf at $6. This would be less forty per cent in cash, or less twenty-five per cent if using credit. As a member of the Baker Street Irregulars and the author of a little volume called *On Conan Doyle*, I tend to check out anything relating to Sherlock Holmes or his creator. But I left this book: the binding was loose and the covers stained. Besides, I already owned *Adventures of Gerard* in both the American and English editions. Had it been a prettier copy, though, I would have bought it to add to my stash of favourites I like to give as presents.

A truly responsible collector would carry a list of his wants or even a tablet computer containing a bibliographical database of everything he owns. I disdain such librarianship. I know, more or less, what books I possess, with a fairly accurate idea of their condition. Most are hardcovers, and usually, though not exclusively, first editions. What matters to me is that the fiction be of the period of its initial publication and that secondary texts—author biographies, collections of essays, scholarly commentaries—be the best of their kind. Given my druthers, I prefer pages displaying a reasonably large type font on reasonably good paper. A dust jacket is welcome but not compulsory, since I confess to an ineradicable fondness for worn book cloth and elaborately decorated bindings.

That Friday, I gathered in relatively short order a small selection from the warehouse's regular shelves: T.H. White's *Book of Beasts* in a jacket, Edgar Wallace's *The Just Men of Cordova*—to round out my set of the Just Men adventures—and an omnibus of three Elizabeth Daly mysteries, two of them featuring her rare book expert Henry Gamadge. In the store's "Books on Books" section, I picked up *Printing and the Mind of Man: Catalogue of the Exhibitions at the British Museum and at Earls Court, London, 16–27 July 1963*. Those two complementary shows, organized by the legendary bookmen John Carter, Stanley Morison and Percy Muir, highlighted not only key titles in the history of civilization—many items lent by Ian Fleming from his personal library—but also the tools and equipment used to print them. While I own the later, oversized hardcover of *PMM*, the original guide to the exhibitions seemed attractive on its own and worth $8, less discount. A collector should always trust his or her instincts. As I later discovered, however, the catalogue isn't particularly scarce or valuable. Still, if I hadn't seen it physically in front of me, I might never have known of its existence—still another reason to support your local bricks-and-mortar bookstore.

With noon now fast approaching, I finally decided to transfer scouting operations to the adjoining sale annexe. What if the snow started early? In this area of the warehouse the double- and triple-shelved bargain books aren't categorized. Occasionally one runs across a cluster of works devoted to, say, pirates, or rows of Judaica, or even entire bookcases filled with ponderous tomes in German. Otherwise, it's a matter of simply scanning every title. To assist my aged eyes, I always carry a little flashlight to illuminate darkened spines on shadowy lower shelves.

On one of these last I noticed two dozen volumes of the English Men of Letters series, matching thin maroon volumes from the late nineteenth century. Some were firsts, some not. I went through them all and kept four, largely because of the author rather than the subject: Mark Pattison on Milton, John Addington Symonds on Shelley, R.C. Jebb on Richard Bentley, and Anthony Trollope on Thackeray. Part of me now feels I should have taken the lot. Having long ago read the Jebb and Trollope, I know those volumes are special—an important classicist on the greatest of all classicists, a major novelist on the master he most revered—while the others are largely examples of outmoded Victorian scholarship. Still, the set did look so pretty en masse...

By the time the snow actually began to fall, I'd made quite a pile of $2 books, all of them in jackets: *Art and Psychoanalysis*, edited by William Phillips, Augustus John's memoir *Chiaroscuro*, Nicholas Monsarrat's *The Boy's Book of the Sea*, Peter Hopkirk's *Like Hidden Fire* (still another approach to the "Great Game" in Central Asia), W.M. Spackman's *An Armful of Warm Girl*, a short novel as eccentrically original in its style as in its brilliant title, and *The Second Cuckoo*, a compendium of cranky and funny letters to *The Times* which I couldn't pass up since *The First Cuckoo* already reposed on my night stand. As for *The God That Failed*, the once famous book in which Arthur Koestler, Ignazio Silone, Richard Wright, André Gide, Louis Fischer (who he?) and Stephen Spender "confess" why they joined, then left the Communist Party, that surely was worth the price of a small Starbucks coffee. Finally, just as I was about to hurry home, I plucked forth a yellow-jacketed book that turned out to be Philip Larkin's *Jill*, published by the Overlook Press in 1976. Despite the late date, it's actually the first American edition and was in quite good nick. Larry McMurtry's bookstore in Archer City wanted $300 for a comparable copy.

While Second Story's warehouse is certainly a treasure house, I would be remiss not to mention an even more Aladdin-like cave of wonders an hour west of Washington. Wonder Book and Video comprises three Maryland stores owned by Chuck Roberts—in Frederick, Hagerstown and Gaithersburg—and a behemoth warehouse and mailing depot the size of a football field. You could fit half a dozen Second Story Warehouses inside. Only friends and special customers are generally allowed in, however. On my all too rare visits, I like best to pick through the several rooms of spillover "vintage" material. I once found two odd volumes from the *New English Dictionary*, as the *Oxford English Dictionary* was called when it was first being issued in parts. They were, as I happened to remember, just the two volumes lacking from my friend John Clute's broken set, bought by him in London forty years earlier. I had Chuck ship them the next day.

It was the least I could do. After all, it was Clute who introduced me to the most exhilarating booking I've ever known, judging on a volume-per-minute basis. On misty Saturday mornings in 1980s London, all the city's runners and a few mad collectors would congregate around the canvas-covered book barrows on Farringdon Road. When George Jeffery, with a flourish, pulled away the tarp from one of his trestles at 9 a.m., the table would be swept bare in twenty seconds or less. On my first visit, a novice among the professionals, I nonetheless scored two bound volumes of the *Strand* magazine containing the first six Sherlock Holmes adventures. They set me back all of fifty pence each.

If I'm not mistaken, I now seem to be growing distinctly garrulous, as book collectors often do when they start to reminisce. Instead, let me end where I began. When I got home from Second Story that wintry Friday, the snowstorm had begun in earnest. I ate some of the home-made chicken soup my wife had left me, then sat back in a chair with a glass of wine and watched the thickly falling flakes. I felt serene, wonderfully at peace. Still, that quiet contentment, I knew, wouldn't last for long. Once the snow cleared, it would be time to check out the Friends of the Montgomery County Library Bookstore in nearby Wheaton. Who knows what might show up there? Why, once I found an almost mint copy of... But I really should tell you about it some other time.

Dussmann:
A Conversation

DANIEL KEHLMANN

First Man: Can we talk about the book trade?

Second Man: Do we have to?

First Man: I'm afraid so. We're writers, after all. And we're readers too. We live off it, in many respects.

Second Man: Theoretically.

First Man: What do you mean theoretically—we live off the sales of books!

Second Man: Not necessarily. I live off giving readings and talks. Also teaching sometimes. I teach people who want to write books how to write books that sell so well that you can live off them. I do that because my books don't sell so well that I can live off them.

First Man: If the bookshops were better, you could live off them.

Second Man: It's nice of you not to say that I could do it if my books were better. But the bookshops aren't to blame, they really aren't. Not the big ones, not the small ones.

FIRST MAN: I love the really small bookshops.

SECOND MAN: Oh, me too.

FIRST MAN: The tiny shops where the owner speaks to each customer personally, full of passion and a sense of mission.

SECOND MAN: Fabulous.

FIRST MAN: I'm glad that they still exist.

SECOND MAN: Me too.

FIRST MAN: But I don't like to go to them.

SECOND MAN: Me neither.

FIRST MAN: I actually don't want anyone to speak to me.

SECOND MAN: Full of passion and a sense of mission. No, I don't want that either. I don't need it. I have a sense of mission myself.

FIRST MAN: Really?

SECOND MAN: Yes. No. Whatever. I don't know whether I have it. Anyway, passion and a sense of mission are inherently good things.

FIRST MAN: Very much so.

SECOND MAN: But I don't need that. What I like is…

FIRST MAN: Yeah?

SECOND MAN: Well, I like to be left in peace. I really like that a lot.

FIRST MAN: Yeah, to be left in peace, that's a wonderful thing.

SECOND MAN: And that's why I like Dussmann.

FIRST MAN: The huge cultural department store in Mitte, the extremely ugly central district of Berlin?

Second Man: That's the one.

First Man: You live nearby, don't you?

Second Man: Oh yes.

First Man: Awful area.

Second Man: Really awful. In Mitte no one praises Berlin's charm. The Friedrichstrasse train station is there, the streams of tourists are there, the employees of parliament and public television are there on their way to work or to their conspiratorial lunches at the taxpayer's expense. Dussmann fits in there. Dussmann doesn't have any charm either. But Dussmann has books.

First Man: Three floors full.

Second Man: Four floors, four! Not to mention the movies in the basement. Incredible quantities of books. Everything thoroughly organized, everything makes sense. When you look for something, you find it.

First Man: The way foreigners imagine Germany.

Second Man: And the way Germany in reality hardly is nowadays. The trains are always late, the large construction sites are never finished, and you can't get an appointment at the local administrative office due to overload. I know people who can't get married because they can't get an appointment there. Unless you're marrying someone who works at the office, then it's quick. These days Germany is as disorganized as any country in Central or Eastern Europe.

First Man: Except at Dussmann.

SECOND MAN: Right. At Dussmann order prevails. Four floors—

FIRST MAN: And a basement with movies.

SECOND MAN: Four floors full of books, everywhere red wall-to-wall carpets, well-arranged display tables, perfect organization. I haven't found out about new releases from newspapers for a long time, I've found out about them from the Dussmann display tables on which they are well arranged. You find everything here, and what you don't find, the competent employees show you. When I was looking in the comics section recently for the second volume of the comic version of Tove Jansson's *Moomin* books—a work that probably isn't asked for every day—the employee was able to tell me its exact location on the shelf without having to look it up somewhere. And what the competent employees can't show you because it's not there is ordered, and is there the next day.

FIRST MAN: The next day?

SECOND MAN: Yeah, that's even quicker than with—

FIRST MAN: No!

SECOND MAN: With—

FIRST MAN: Don't say the name!

SECOND MAN: Quicker than with the big bad bookseller on the internet. By the way, Dussmann's employees are distinguished by the utmost objectivity. They don't want to chat. They answer questions, they look things up for you. Sometimes they even advise you against something.

Recently an employee in the children's section told me not to buy a certain audio book for my son: "Much too scary for a seven-year-old," she said. She had really listened to it! And when I asked for Hugh Lofting's *Doctor Dolittle* series in the juvenile section, the employee knew immediately and without looking it up that they didn't have it in stock but that there was a *Doctor Dolittle* book in the English section. Such expertise isn't imposed on you at Dussmann, but when you need it, it's available.

FIRST MAN: Is it fair to say that Dussmann is the future of the book trade?

SECOND MAN: I think so. The model of the big chains has failed—inflexible, rarely appealing, always the wrong books in stock, often employees who don't know much. But the small, nice, cosy bookshops with limited space and enthusiastic booksellers can't be the answer. People are used to getting what they want immediately. The answer is therefore: big bookshops that are, however, not part of a chain. That seems to work. With a coffee shop too, as far as I'm concerned. I don't need one, but a lot of people like that, I have nothing against it. What also must be praised about Dussmann, by the way, is the absence of music! It's quiet there! You don't hear anything! That's conducive to concentration and reading, and in my case leads to buying much more than intended. And have I already mentioned that Dussmann is open until midnight? And every day? Even Saturday!

FIRST MAN: You're really enthusiastic.

SECOND MAN: How could you not be enthusiastic: no music, and that until midnight! And no music! There's simply quiet; that's just incredible—quiet!

FIRST MAN: Are there author readings at Dussmann?

SECOND MAN: Of course.

FIRST MAN: How are they?

SECOND MAN: I don't know. They're on a special event stage, far away from the books; you can shop and not catch a word the authors say, isn't that fabulous?

FIRST MAN: You don't like readings?

SECOND MAN: Of course not, I can read on my own. I learned how in school, it's been working great ever since, I read books on my own.

FIRST MAN: Well, it's not only about the reading. Usually authors also explain at readings what they were thinking while writing and whether they work in the morning or in the evening or—

SECOND MAN: But if I don't have the slightest desire to know that, what then? What do I do if it doesn't interest me at all whether they work in the morning or in the evening and if the book is actually enough for me and if I also assume that everything these people say at their readings is inventions and lies anyway—what then?

FIRST MAN: But you yourself give readings!

SECOND MAN: Of course.

FIRST MAN: Why?

SECOND MAN: As I already mentioned, I don't sell enough books not to have to give readings.

First Man: That's the only reason?

Second Man: That's the only reason.

First Man: At Dussmann too?

Second Man: God forbid. I love Dussmann. I don't give readings at Dussmann. I don't want to be a writer at Dussmann, I'm a customer!

First Man: Has Dussmann ever invited you to read?

Second Man: I can say with pride: yes. I would also be a little sad if my favourite bookshop hadn't invited me.

First Man: And you declined?

Second Man: Of course.

First Man: But you read elsewhere?

Second Man: Yes.

First Man: You are a bit odd.

Second Man: Did I mention that I also buy my desk blotters, my pads, my pens, everything I need to be a writer at Dussmann? Not only do they have books, they also have the best stationery section!

First Man: There's one thing I've always wanted to know.

Second Man: Yeah?

First Man: Why is it that at a time when hardly anyone still writes by hand, more notebooks are sold than ever before? All these stationery sections in the bookshops.

Second Man: Writing is simply changing from a cultural technique into a lifestyle thing.

First Man: Not writing. People can't write any more at all. Not by hand. Not with a pen and paper. They don't even have the fine motor skills for it any more.

The muscles in their hands don't play along. No, the lifestyle thing is the purchase of notebooks, which are then left lying around unused.

SECOND MAN: A world in which everyone has empty notebooks lying around at home. Fascinating thesis. Where is Slavoj Žižek when you need him?

FIRST MAN: But we wanted to talk about the future of the book trade. Dussmann isn't a member of a chain. There are no other branches, only this one. That's important. And we wanted to talk about Berlin.

SECOND MAN: That's the same thing.

FIRST MAN: Berlin and Dussmann—the same thing?

SECOND MAN: In terms of atmosphere, absolutely. Cold and impersonal. Uncharming. But still worth visiting and liveable and full of culture, both in the mainstream and at the weirdest fringes, and marked by a high level of education and somehow generally fantastic in the most unobtrusive way. Besides, here's the thing: When you picture a city, you always think of something in particular. You can't simply picture a city in the abstract. And the better you know it, the city, the more specific and personal what you visualize is. When I want to think of Berlin, I usually think fairly quickly of the cultural department store with the red carpets.

FIRST MAN: But Berlin is cool, they say. And Dussmann isn't cool.

SECOND MAN: First of all, I don't know what that's supposed to mean: cool. And if I'm going to pretend I know what it means, I still don't know how a city can be cool. And finally, if I'm going to pretend I could have some clear and distinct image of a cool city, I still have to come right out and say that the idea that Berlin is cool is a brilliant promotional claim for the city, but in reality Berlin is impersonal and ugly and yet, above all, pleasant. You find what you need and what interests you—among things and people and places and possible ways of life.

FIRST MAN: Now you're definitely going to say: like at Dussmann.

SECOND MAN: I am indeed going to say that. Variety and tranquillity, the renunciation of pomp, the objective functionality, and at the same time the widest selection.

FIRST MAN: But that complete absence of atmosphere and charm—

SECOND MAN: Those who want atmosphere should light themselves a candle in their bathroom. And I myself am charming.

FIRST MAN: You think so?

SECOND MAN: Very much so, even. Very charming! And for everything else…

FIRST MAN: Yeah?

SECOND MAN: For everything else, there's Dussmann.

Translated from the German by Ross Benjamin

La Palmaverde

STEFANO BENNI

There's a hole in a colonnade
in the city of Bologna.
Like hell, it swallows young poets.

A benign devil leads them astray.
They emerge transfigured,
crying their verses to the sun.

If outside there is fog,
by some devilry, from the window
of that bookshop you see blue sky.

Books speak even when they are closed.
Lucky the man who can hear
their persistent murmur.

I wrote these lines many years ago. They are dedicated to the poet and intellectual Roberto Roversi, and his bookshop, La Palmaverde, which was one of the cultural miracles of 1970s Italy.

Roversi was a poet, a friend of Pasolini, Leonetti and many others, but he was above all a great example of the passion for literature. His antiquarian bookshop, an old cellar bursting at the seams with tables and bookcases, was the meeting place for Bologna's writers and students. Roversi was a "benign devil", a strange, lively man, loved but also feared for his uncompromising character. Young people approached him with awe and respect, and he dispensed help and advice to all of them. Even though he had offers from many large publishers, he preferred to self-publish his books, either duplicating the copies himself or entrusting them to artisan printers. In the bookshop, apart from all the rare and precious tomes, there were hundreds of slim volumes by poets, from established names to novices. You could often acquire them for a small donation. "There's no price for poetry," he would say, "or if there is, it's not in the money of this world."

I wasn't yet thirty and just starting out as a writer when I first entered the dark, mysterious cave of La Palmaverde.

I was overawed. I roamed around in that semi-darkness, which smelled of paper and inks and was warmed only by an electric heater. But after those first encounters, a beautiful friendship was born. Roversi was my friend and teacher. We talked about everything. Not just about great poetry, but about politics, football, cars, songs: he had written lyrics for the singer-songwriter Lucio Dalla, he wasn't a doctrinaire man of letters, he loved every aspect of life. That was his first lesson: "Whoever said," he would repeat, "that a man of letters has to talk only about literature? That would be like a chef only talking about mayonnaise." And when I took him my first book, with a dedication, he gave me in exchange a volume of his, with these words written in it: "To Stefano who's a writer, a passionate reader, and a good footballer. Continue with all three."

Roberto Roversi died four years ago in respectable poverty, and the bookshop was closed down, much to the indifference of the municipality of Bologna. I'd like to remember him here, starting with some sayings of his that I've never forgotten.

The first saying is: "Books are alive and don't like to be badly treated." La Palmaverde was known around the world, and Roversi sent rare books to a large number of universities in Europe, the United States and Japan. And in order to send them without ruining them, he had become, as he put it, "a great packer". When he had to prepare a parcel of books, he would take hours arranging them one on top of the other, wrapping them first in cardboard, then in high-quality paper, and finally tying the package carefully with string. "It's almost harder to send books on a journey than it is to write them," he would sigh. And he would proudly show me the thank-you letter he had got from a Japanese professor: "Dear Mr Roversi, your expertise as a bookseller is beyond reproach, but above all I have never received packages wrapped with such care or skill." "Can you imagine?" he would say to me with a smile. "A compliment like that from a Japanese! They invented origami!"

The second thing that Roversi often repeated was: "Books choose those who want to buy them."

Roversi only sold if he liked the customer. If the person struck him as unpleasant, pretentious, not a lover of literature, he would immediately regard him with suspicion. I once saw this demonstrated. A smartly dressed gentleman came in and started moving around among the books, leafed through some grudgingly, then pointed to a very expensive art book. "I'd like that one," he said. "It's a present and I want to make a good impression." "I'm sorry," Roversi replied with a sardonic smile, "but that one's already been sold to Professor Nihongi in Tokyo."

And so the customer asked to purchase other books, but each time the desired volume had always been sold to some mysterious character: an English professor called Booker, a French critic named Des Livres, the German bookseller Lohengrin. In the end, the customer left, fuming and empty-handed.

Roberto's third saying was: "Mice don't eat books for no reason."

Among those old and crowded bookshelves, Roversi often had to fight damage from mice and woodworm, and devoted more than one poem to them. "They aren't enemies," he would say, "just somewhat intrusive colleagues. When a mouse eats a book, it's because the paper is of good quality, the mould on it is tasty, or else because the writing is excellent. Beware of books that the mice avoid!"

The last sentence I remember is: "Books are so full of thoughts that some of them have learned to think." And he recalled the incident involving a precious edition of the *Divine Comedy*, a heavy tome that mysteriously fell three times from the high shelf where it had been placed. There must be a reason, Roversi said, and he soon discovered it.

"You see," he told me, "I'd put that *Divine Comedy* next to a nineteenth-century book celebrating the life of Pope Boniface VIII. And as you know, Dante considered that pontiff his worst enemy, so much so that he consigned him to hell. That's the reason for those strange falls: that *Divine Comedy* preferred to jump rather than rub shoulders with a book glorifying its adversary!"

That was La Palmaverde, a place of culture but also of craftsmanship and hard work. Roberto still wrote out the lists and categorization of the books by hand. One day, his wife persuaded him to buy a computer. He looked at it with curiosity then said, "All right, let's modernize. But only you will use it. Just promise me one thing: that if you want to know where a book is, you'll ask me, not the computer. I'm jealous."

The fact is, he had an incredible memory and could find his way through that maze of titles at great speed. He carried an iron stepladder on his shoulder and would climb it to get to the tops of packed shelves that touched the ceiling. He knew where almost all the books were, in which bookcase or in which drawer. And above all, he had his cabinet of favourite books, a hundred beloved titles. Thanks to him, I realized that the passion for literature is an infinite *aleph*, in which we are dramatically linked to all the stories and books in the world. But then we choose the *hapax*, our uniqueness as readers and writers.

He wrote his poetry with a pen, or sometimes on a typewriter that rattled like a machine gun. Once he showed me a manuscript of his, so full of marks and crossings-out as to be almost illegible. "You see?" he said. "This is the history of my doubts." From him I learned that writing is searching, trying again, improving. "We read and reread," Roversi would say, "but above all we write and rewrite. I don't trust a writer who does a book in a few months, without thoroughly revising it."

But when I admitted to him that I was working on a book and had rewritten some pages more than fifty times, he smiled and said, "Maybe you should stop now. There comes a time when your work is over and it starts belonging to other people."

You didn't go to La Palmaverde just to talk about high literature. You also went there to enjoy yourself, to play cards, to have a snack of bread and mortadella. Above all, Roversi loved practical jokes, especially if he found some gullible person or fake expert. He would invent imaginary titles, phantom books, improbable writers. We invented a poet, René Nexistepas: a customer heard us talking about him admiringly, fell for it, and ordered all his books. He came back several times to pay for them, and each time Roversi would apologize with comical humility: "It's a scandal, they haven't sent us any René Nexistepas this week either, I'm so sorry..."

Roversi paid an exorbitant rent, and made a lot of sacrifices to keep the bookshop going. When he realized that the owner of the building was about to evict him, and that nobody in the city council would help, he devised one last joke.

We started to circulate the rumour that there was an old treasure hidden in La Palmaverde. Somewhere behind the walls of books was a passage that led to a secret room, where something of enormous value was kept.

The owner of the building got to hear about this rumour, and on the pretext of checking the state of the premises, he began paying visits. He would roam around between the bookcases, tap the walls in search of a hollow space, search in every corner. Eventually we left a key in full view on a desk for him to find. With it was a note saying:

Key to the red door. Enter only if absolutely necessary. There you will find the precious marble throne.

The trick worked. The owner of the building found the little red door at the end of a narrow corridor. While we pretended to make conversation, we heard him turn the key in the lock and go in.

He found himself in a little room with a toilet bowl: the bookshop's lavatory.

He slammed the door as he left.

This was Roversi, and this was his weird and wonderful old bookshop. I loved those dark rooms smelling of mould much more than modern bookshops full of lights and screens.

In the poem with which I opened, I called La Palmaverde "hell". Because I recall a conversation I had with that magical bookseller.

Literature (and its shrine, the bookshop) is a breeding ground for ideas forged in the flames of creation and the fire of rewriting. Books are about good and evil, and about being condemned, willingly, to descend ever further into the depths of the soul. In heaven, everything is perfect, nothing can be improved, everything is already written in a beautiful hand, without corrections or second thoughts. That's why the destiny of literature is closer to a hell filled with wonderful torments than a heaven full of satisfaction.

La Palmaverde no longer exists. But its books, its words and its lesson are still out there in the world, and inside my head.

Translated from the Italian by Howard Curtis

A Bookshop in
the Age of Progress

Pankaj Mishra

F act and Fiction Bookshop began life in the early 1980s in a corner of a market in Vasant Vihar in South Delhi. I first visited it one afternoon in September 1989. A morose-looking man in his thirties sat hunched over a tiny desk, surrounded by neat piles of new paperbacks that rose to his waist. He looked up when I came in, and then immediately hung his head again.

I had heard about the shop and its owner, Ajit Vikram Singh, from a friend at my university. Word of his aloof manner had got around; it implied feudal privilege and an education at some elite establishment. I, on the other hand, felt my poverty and isolation acutely in those days, fearing that my clothes betrayed my lack of status. I was glad of his lack of scrutiny as I entered.

It was a small bookshop, no bigger than an average bedroom. But on that first day I was there for hours, barely able to look up from the rows and rows of carefully curated books.

I had spent most of my life in places where the word "bookshop" referred to the place that sold school textbooks and stationery, or to the little bookstall at railway and bus stations: retailers, exclusively, of crime, porn and self-help. Some variety was offered by mobile bookshops, subsidized by the Soviet Union, which toured small towns, offering subscriptions to Soviet magazines and organizing book fairs where you could buy two hardback editions of Russian classics for Rs 5 (at a time when $1 equalled Rs 18).

These bookshops stocked translations of left-wing internationalist writers like Pablo Neruda, Lu Xun, and Nazim Hikmet. Gorky and Mayakovsky—heroes of the revolution—were much preferred, and Soviet pride in the Nobel laureate Sholokhov was expressed through multiple editions of *And Quiet Flows the Don*. But you wouldn't have encountered Bulgakov, Mandelstam or Akhmatova.

In the years since my childhood, I had often come across the names of these writers not favoured, and even persecuted, by the Soviet regime. I had read about their life and work; and now here were all their books.

Fact and Fiction was a bookshop—increasingly rare in India—of surprises and discoveries: where the lesser-known Ivan Klíma nestled along with Milan Kundera, and Carlos Fuentes and Maxine Hong Kingston were as well represented as Gabriel García Márquez and Amy Tan. Harvill's translations of European classics—Leonardo Sciascia, Elio Vittorini—complemented the more conventional fare from Penguin. There were also books from the United

States—Vintage and Pantheon editions of Michel Foucault and Edward Said—which were rarely seen in India, part of the British-dominated Commonwealth marketplace of books.

I had just moved that summer of 1989 to Jawaharlal Nehru University (JNU). I was registered as a graduate student in English. But unlike my peers who came to the university— one of the best Indian institutions in the humanities—to seek a career in academia or in the civil service, I had little interest in a formal education or a degree.

During a life spent in small towns where nothing happened, I had become addicted to random reading (and a bit of furtive writing). And I was already twenty, long past the age when most Indians start to define their professional trajectories.

I sought at JNU nothing more than some more years of idleness subsidized by my parents (and the Indian government).

The university offered the best facilities in this regard. It had a well-stocked library, with many European classics. The room at the dormitory was bigger and cleaner than any I had known. The food was consistently good and cheap. And then I discovered Fact and Fiction, less than a mile away from JNU.

My inability to afford most non-Soviet books had made me an ardent bibliophile. I pored over publishing catalogues that I picked up at Delhi's book fair and marvelled at their diverse plenitude of enjoyment and instruction. Now, here were many of those books, suddenly accessible, if not affordable.

I returned often to the bookshop in the following weeks until I had committed the shelves to memory. The bookseller remained mute and unmoving, enclosed by his mini skyscrapers of books. I didn't mind. I hoped to move quietly through the world, sticking close to the things that brought me contentment.

The bookshop's proximity helped me carve out my own little private geography on the large and daunting map of Delhi. As a young man from the provinces I had been immediately impressed by the city. And on the face of it Delhi offered plenty of scope for new adventures, possibilities of growth. There were, in well-protected enclaves, libraries and bookshops; the cultural sections of foreign embassies hosted film festivals and book readings.

But I lacked both the money and confidence to enjoy them more than occasionally—to not feel a small shock after emerging into a humid night from the cool auditorium of the British Council onto the broken pavement with the limbless beggars. The promise of the metropolis's cultural excitements then felt hollow; it seemed a setting not for pleasure and growth but for work and struggle.

The cosily air-conditioned and usually deserted bookshop in Vasant Vihar seemed to have all I wanted from a metropolis. Little did I know then that it was also a refuge for its owner. After a few weeks of silence, Ajit opened up, offering me coffee, and told me a bit about himself. Privately educated in one of India's best schools and one of its best colleges, he had joined his family's agricultural business before realizing it was not for him—a reader and a bibliophile, who felt happiest among books.

Still, opening a bookshop in an office complex in what was then a remote corner of Delhi was a business gamble. He could not depend on indigent students like myself. Visitors to the Priya Cinema opposite the bookshop, which showed soft pornographic films, could not be trusted to walk out without a book tucked in their trousers. His most regular customers were diplomats living in Vasant Vihar.

Ajit complained incessantly about the book industry: ignorant sales reps, who did not know the difference between Isabel Allende and Marguerite Duras. He spent most of his day scanning catalogues of international publishing houses, highlighting titles he wanted for his shop, and then pursuing his orders through a recalcitrant bureaucracy.

All this arduous curation made him impatient with visitors to the shop, mostly affluent people in expensive clothes, who wanted discounts on books with already very low or marked-down prices. He would look up, his face impassive, and then simply say, "No." I noticed over time that his responses ranged in severity. Those asking for greeting cards or the bestseller of the day met with pure contempt. He said nothing at all to people who failed to recall the title or the name of the author and vaguely offered, "It's about elephants…"

He would cry out, as though in pain, if he saw someone mishandling a book. I shared his outrage. As the months passed, my days came to be organized around visits to the bookshop; and I felt a bit proprietorial about its wares.

Ajit seemed happy for me to use his bookshop as a library or sorts. But I wanted actually to be his customer rather than a mere browser. (Though dedicated to advancing socialism, the Soviet-subsidized bookshops with their cheap offerings had infected me with the neuroses of private ownership.)

In the past, I had saved money on my meals to buy the few books I possessed. There were few such opportunities for self-denial at JNU. I had to wait for a windfall—a birthday present or a Diwali gift from my parents or sisters, who had started to work.

As my savings grew I found them outpaced by my desire to buy a three-volume Vintage US edition of *Remembrance of Things Past*, which I saw advertised in a catalogue that Ajit regularly perused. I had already read Proust in a Penguin Classics edition borrowed from an older friend in Allahabad. But this seemed, in the classic mental inflation of the besotted consumer, something superior: the Scott Moncrieff translation revised by Terence Kilmartin.

It took me a few visits to summon up the courage to ask Ajit if he would order the volumes for me. I could only pay for them in instalments, I said. Much to my delight, he agreed. I still remember the weeks of anticipation leading up to the moment when I saw the volumes in their hard case at the shop, and the pure ecstasy with which I carried them back to my room and smelled the pages.

My own indulgence in sensuous consumerism was no coincidence. The Soviet Union had already imploded, perestroika and glasnost bringing down the shutters on Soviet-subsidized bookshops in India. A shop selling greeting cards replaced a Communist bookshop I used to visit in Delhi. The Indian middle classes were moving away from decades of economic protectionism and virtuous austerity; they had started to embrace unselfconsciously the culture of consumption.

The market around Fact and Fiction registered these changes. The first sign was the Priya Cinema turning into a multiplex. A pastry shop opened, followed by a supermarket selling imported cheeses, where the youngest members of a rising affluent class could be seen savouring their growing wealth. Their glowingly clear skin tones and brand-name jeans and sneakers, their emblems of class as well as caste, gave the market a touch of glamour, and made me anxious about the future of Ajit's venture.

In the 1990s, my search for a perfect retreat took me to a village in the Himalayan state of Himachal Pradesh, nearly a day's journey from Delhi. In my serenely unhurried time there, I started to write more regularly, and to publish book reviews in Indian periodicals. The fees were meagre, but sufficient for me to buy a book or two a month. I always returned to Delhi with some eagerly hoarded cash and mounting excitement. I would go straight to Fact and Fiction to find Ajit hunched morosely as always over his desk, but keen to show me his latest acquisitions.

As the years passed, I was also able to afford more of his books, and have them mailed to my Himalayan home. I plucked them out of the shelves, and watched with pleasure my personal pile of books rise on the floor around Ajit's desk. I was now, finally, a regular customer.

I also developed another bond with the bookshop. The publisher for Penguin in Delhi noticed my book reviews, and wrote to ask if I would write a book for him. Flattered, I immediately suggested a travel book on Indian small towns, which, I suspected, had become with the growth of social aspiration the crucible for India's political and cultural transformation.

It was hard for me to leave my village, and travel to tourist-addled Shimla just ten miles away, let alone imagine myself picking my way through the squalor of small-town India. But the desire to write a book and become a published author, which had barely expressed itself during my years of random reading and scribbling, suddenly seemed close to fulfilment. For six months I travelled around India, using various modes of transport—buses, cars, trains and, once, a ferry.

During my travels I discovered that the placid small-town India of my books-filled childhood had all but disappeared—the family-planning slogans, such as *Hum Do Hamare Do* ("Two of Us, Two We Have"), as well as the framed pictures of Gandhi exhorting austere living; Indrajal and Amar Chitra Katha comics substituted for Superman and Batman; and Rasna powder and Rooh Afza sherbet to slake our thirst for sugary colas.

The Indian economy, liberalized in 1991, now offered, together with religious nationalism and satellite television, to bridge the gap between desire and consummation, where I had previously lived. There was less need for local substitutes, let alone books, and a culture of reflection and reading. Images invoking the world's richness—its great material plenitude—were suddenly everywhere: in billboards promising to equip the nuclear family with multiple cars and also palatial houses with private guards.

My book, describing the darkly ambiguous progress of the New India, came out, and, much to my surprise, did well. The next time I went to Fact and Fiction it was displayed in the window. Ajit told me that a lot of people had asked for it. Over the next twenty years, I would return to the bookshop each time I published a book for the immense thrill of seeing it in the window, chosen from among many on the shelves that I had once longed to possess.

Ajit's mood, however, was grimmer each time I saw him. He complained a lot more about the retail trade, increasingly dominated by execrably written bestsellers for young adults, and about the commercial rents in the area, which were rising steeply, squeezing his profits. A chain book-shop had opened in the vicinity, threatening to drive him out of the market. E-retailers like Amazon and Flipkart had increased the number of people looking up cheaper bargains on smartphones.

Literary festivals with internationally famous writers, which grew exponentially in India, did little to boost book sales; they were, he said, celebrity peep shows. Young read-ers, addicted to mass-market fiction and self-help titles pro-duced by a handful of writers, showed no signs of growing up and moving on to more nutritious fare. India's very few independent bookshops were rapidly going out of business.

Yet Ajit was as determined as ever to keep his shop free of non-literary offerings and greeting cards. Little did I know that he was running out of time. A couple of years ago, a friend—among the many I had introduced to Ajit—told me that the bookshop's "days are numbered". The expression felt callous, but it did at least prepare me for the news last year that Ajit had finally decided to close his bookshop.

I was in Delhi then, and thought of visiting Fact and Fiction, but then I saw an article by Ajit on a news website. He said he was proud when his old clients came into the shop with their children, and told them how the bookshop was "an integral part of their formative years". "They actually thank me!" he wrote.

But then he added: "For the past several years, I have spent hours wondering what has happened to my dream profession. Where have my loyal clients gone? Where have the friendships, forged over the counter discussing the joys of reading and discovering old and new books, vanished?"

Reading this, I thought I couldn't go back. I felt guilty about my own prolonged absences from the bookshop, and about the fact that I had been reading a lot more on Kindle, participating in effect in the general undermining of bricks-and-mortar bookshops.

Furthermore, there had been harsh reminders in recent months that reading and writing literary fiction and non-fiction are dispensable luxuries of a tiny minority. A malign and often murderous political movement—Hindu nationalism—had started to target intellectuals and artists. Writers had been assassinated or assaulted, with banning and public bonfires of books and death threats by demagogues. They seemed horribly exposed to the rage of the left-behind, the frustrations of the overambitious, and the contempt of the rich.

Fact and Fiction closed in late 2015. Ajit called it a "mercy killing" in one of the many articles that appeared. He seemed relieved. I shared his unsentimental mood. Bookshops still give me a frisson when I pass them on the street, even though I know they do not—cannot—hold the riches that the young provincial in me found at Fact and Fiction one afternoon in 1989.

It is also true that we had both been refugees from a frantically "developing" country, whose priorities of economic growth and individual aggrandizement did not include, and possibly deliberately excluded, an intellectual and literary culture.

So many landmarks had disappeared since I first visited the bookshop that humid day in 1989, and daydreamed about owning the three volumes of Proust. India has been on a relentless march of progress since then. The destination has grown less clear, and the way ahead looks even more arduous. But this is how the "angel of history" moves, as Walter Benjamin once wrote: the storm of progress that smashes everything in its way driving him relentlessly into the future, while "the pile of debris before him grows toward the sky".

Intimacy

DORTHE NORS

... a book is more than a verbal structure or series of verbal structures; it is the dialogue it establishes with its reader and the intonation it imposes upon his voice and the changing and durable images it leaves in his memory.

—Jorge Luis Borges
"Note on (toward) Bernard Shaw"

I t's summer, I think. Through Grandma's windows I can see the terraced houses across the street. The hedges that border the front yards have yellow blossoms; I know they're called cinquefoils. An old coffee-stained book lies on the low table. It's much too warm here, for Grandma doesn't dare open windows. It's the draught; it goes right into her side. The pain runs from a spot under her ribs, up under her shoulder blades and so to her neck. She says it makes her entire face tense. So we're not allowed to open the windows, and I'm sitting on the couch, which is moss green and striped. On the front of the book are two girls' names and a woman in robes standing erect. One of the names has written the book, the other's its subject. I'm twelve, maybe thirteen, and I don't know who's who, and now Grandma comes back from the bedroom. She's been to fetch the last two volumes. *Since I can no longer read them, you may as well have them*, she says. The books jostle her coffee cup when she sets them down, but one coffee stain more or less makes no difference. The books have been read to tatters. *I was also bad about lending them out*, Grandma says.

The reason I'm to have them is that reading books makes Grandma's neck hurt; she can't tolerate sitting with something in her hands, and she also says that all the flies have vanished from the face of the earth. Back when they lived out on the farm, when Grandpa was alive, there were flies everywhere. She says that since she moved to town, the flies have disappeared. *Could well be that hole in the ozone*, Grandma says, and I think it could also be that we're not allowed to open the windows. *So I've read them for the last time*, she says with a sigh, placing her hand upon the stack. *It was Bookman Erichsen, you know, who got me to buy them.*

It's as if her age is shifting inside her. She's no longer Grandma but the woman she was before. She's looking out of the window, and if her gaze weren't so blurred by the dissolution of time, it'd be the cinquefoil she was looking at. *He was a tall man*, she says, *Bookman Erichsen. It was a classy shop to step into. No clutter on the shelves. And I knew of course where to find Morten Korch. He was on the left when you entered, and he was who we read, Grandpa and I. What we would do is that Grandpa would lie down on the divan, and then I'd sit down in the chair beside it, and then I'd read from Morten Korch while we had coffee. That was in the evenings.*

I'm twelve, maybe thirteen years old, and I'm familiar with Morten Korch. He wrote books about and for country people. In them everything was idyllic, and distinctions black and white, and in the fifties his books were made into movies. Danes crowded into the darkness of movie theatres to see Korch's romantic portraits of farm life. During most of my childhood, the TV showed a Korch film every Saturday night to entertain a little nation, a people that was starting to lose its roothold. But before these nights on TV, Korch's books had been regular fare in their small homes, and Grandma had sat under a kerosene lamp and read page after page about how good it was to be a farmer, while Grandpa had lain arthritic on the divan and listened. *Of course I was always able to find the Korch shelf at Erichsen's on my own*, says Grandma. *But then one day Erichsen was suddenly standing there in person. White shirt, black jacket, and he must have been married, for his trousers were creased. You could really tell he was someone who wanted to do something for his customers. It was almost embarrassing*, says Grandma, though she doesn't mean it. She's smiling in any case, and it's summer, and something is blooming in her mind's eye. *Then I said to Erichsen I was just going to see if there was anything new from Korch, and Erichsen said, "There's always something new from Korch, even though Korch has nothing new to say,"* and then he cocked his head a bit to the side and said I ought to stop reading such crap. *Very shiny shoes he had, and elegant, and then he bent over me and said,*

"May I, ma'am?" And I had no clue what it was he was asking, so I blushed.

Grandma holds a hand up before her eyes. Now she's alone for a moment with herself and Erichsen, and then I can tell she's back: *He said I should challenge my excellent brain. He said he had books that would do something to me, and then he found* Kristin Lavransdatter *by Sigrid Undset. He had the whole trilogy, but I'd been sent into town by Grandpa to buy Korch. We dug the potatoes up in the autumn, you know. The rows were terribly long, and when your father was a boy, he cried when we set him at the end of a row and told him he'd have to keep digging till he reached the far end. You should have seen our hands when we'd come in at night. We couldn't grip anything, and our nails would be all torn up, and then Grandpa would want to be read to. It bored the children, for then they weren't allowed to speak in front of him. The radio had to be turned off too, and then he'd lie there and stare at the damp stain on the ceiling while I read about the big open barns and the wagons loaded high. But then it was Erichsen thought I should buy* Kristin Lavransdatter *instead. "It's the sort of a book you won't soon forget, ma'am." I didn't manage to tell him that my husband would probably disagree, because Erichsen was too busy leafing through pages and explaining. He touched me lightly on the elbow and talked about Sigrid Undset. About Norway. And feminine forces, good Lord.*

Grandma's got stumpy old legs. She wears nylon stockings, and her dress is always polyester. When you touch her, she rustles synthetically; the lenses of her glasses are smudged. She's over eighty, and Grandpa and Erichsen are both long dead. *But then I bought them*, Grandma says, fumbling with the first volume till she's lifted it free of the coffee table. *And that's something I could never explain to anyone: what it was like to ride the bus home with no Morten Korch.*

Something is happening behind Grandma's small locked face. There's a sorrow in there, yet beside it pride as well over something I'm too young to understand, and yet I understand that it's Erichsen who's put it there. We become the person someone imagines we are, and now the books are mine; or we become what we read, and Erichsen's Bookshop was borne along by a belief that we can grow away from the place we've always been forced to stand. We have the potential to become greater than the role we've been expected to play. To set this growth in motion requires affection and respect for the human being as a phenomenon—and the growth can be triggered by a bookseller's interested and learned presence. I know this because I visited the bookshop myself for many years afterward. Overseen by the man who succeeded Erichsen, and the man who succeeded him, but as we sat there in Grandma's flat I was twelve, maybe thirteen. It was summer, I think; the cinquefoil was blooming. I didn't know what I was supposed to do with the old books. They were yellowed and smelled of bedrooms and dust. Fingers had dog-eared the pages and frayed the edges. The spines had long since cracked and separated. *How am I supposed to take care of them?* I thought. *And what is it I'm supposed to take care of? Three books? Or something in Grandma?* I didn't know, though I had a suspicion, and then I turn fourteen, turn fifteen, turn sixteen and still I don't touch *Kristin Lavransdatter*. I can't read books that have been read so mercilessly, and I haul Sigrid and Kristin through one flat after another. I study literature at the university, I write, I publish my first novel, and one day in 2003 Grandma dies, nearly one hundred years old. I've lied to her for decades. I've said, *Oh yes, I've read* Kristin Lavransdatter, every time she asked. But I haven't read *Kristin Lavransdatter*. I managed to get a master's in Nordic literature and wander through one literary situation after another without having read *Kristin Lavransdatter*. Yet I still have the books. They're in a box in a storage room, and I don't know what I'm supposed to do with them, now Grandma's no longer alive. I can't throw them away.

And then it happens. I'm in my late thirties and have settled in Copenhagen, infinitely far from the potato fields of central Jutland. My grandfather no longer asks for release from reality, Grandma no longer pines, and I've just written a short story collection. It's called *Karate Chop*, and now it's out in the shops. I'm walking down Gammel Kongevej in Copenhagen. It's winter, I think. My feet are cased in black boots, my hands have vanished into gloves, and I can see my breath before me as I step lightly through the cold. The stories have been favourably reviewed, I'm feeling proud, and on the far side of the intersection there lies a bookshop. It looks small and cosy, but I've never been inside before. I get an urge to go into it and see if my stories are there. Across the street and into the warmth: a bell rings as I enter.

My eyes have to adjust to the dim light, but then I see the counter, and the woman behind it. She's not young, and her cardigan is buttoned up her chest. I say I'm just browsing. She nods, and I walk over to the bookcase with new releases. The tip of my index finger glides affectionately past L and M, and then I come to N, where my book stands. Seeing your work on a bookshop shelf never stops being meaningful, and even though I have a crate of author's comps standing in my flat, I still have to touch this *actual* copy. I take the book from the shelf, open it, thumb through it, read the jacket copy, and imagine I'm some unfamiliar customer in this bookshop, considering whether to buy this book. It's the sort of slim book that easily disappears on a shelf. Which is to say that it's easy to overlook, and I do so want for people to see it, to leaf through it and quicken with interest. What I do then is not to put the book back in its place. Instead, I place it facing outward on the edge of the shelf. I place it on display—on exhibit, in short—and I smile a little shyly as I do so. It's as if I'm showing my nakedness to strangers. It's a silly act, but there's something tender in it, at least I think so, and then I hurry over to another shelf. Take a book, check the price, and walk to the till with a girlish smile on my lips.

And then she stands there, the older woman behind the counter. She's not tall, and I set the book down, saying, *It's a lovely shop.* She nods. I say, *Yes, I actually write a bit myself.* It's embarrassing to say, but I can't help but say it, and she doesn't respond. I say, *In fact, I was just over by the new releases to look at a book of mine. I couldn't help but place it with the cover facing out.* I laugh. *One can be so nutty sometimes.* And then I glance from the book the woman is putting in a little bag up to the woman's face, and it is severe: *Have you been going and moving books around my store?* she wants to know. I say, *Round and round, it's still in the N's.* She steps out from behind the counter and squeezes past me; I catch a faint whiff of lavender. Outside the shop it's begun to snow, and the woman, clad in nylon tights, skirt and sensible shoes, is heading over to the N's. She stands on tiptoe, grabs my book, and then stuffs it roughly back into the shelf. *Do you have any idea how many authors I get scurrying through my shop?* she says as she edges past me again. *You all just want to be seen and touched*, she says. *But when you move books around, then I can't find them again, and then I can't sell you!*

I'm upholstered from the inside out against the Scandinavian winter, and yet at the same time I'm standing there stark naked. I try to defend myself from the woman's gaze, for she's calling into question both my integrity and my very being. She doesn't want to touch or be touched by me, doesn't want to see or be seen by me. She doesn't want to be in the same room. She says, *Out of my shop.*

I say, *What's that?* She says, *You heard me. Out!* I say, *But you can't just do that.* She says, *I can do what I want, they're my premises.*

Fortunately there's a green man at the crossing outside. It's snowing, and I'm leaving the scene of the crime with my little bag. I don't make it any farther than the bakery by the intersection at City Hall before I let myself cry. I don't want to stop walking, for it's winter; all the faces I pass are twisted in grimaces, and I go as fast as I can through the park, home to my street, in the main door and up to the fifth floor: the shame.

I have a hard time getting the sobbing under control. And the anger. I walk around and sound like a kid sneering at a playmate, *She can't do that!* The two of us were supposed to be playing the same game, and I thought of course she understood; but instead, I ended up making myself vulnerable, and she ended up punishing me for it. A bit of internal bleeding has occurred, a break in confidence, and when I've cursed my throat dry, I make up my mind that the woman in the shop on Gammel Kongevej should know, so I sit down to the computer and write:

Dear proprietor,

I was in your establishment today, and you threw me out for reasons you no doubt recall. I want to tell you about my grandmother and a man named Erichsen. He was a bookseller in Jutland. One day she stepped into his shop to buy some genre fiction to read aloud to my worn-down grandfather. But Erichsen knew his calling, and so he convinced her to buy a great work of literature by Sigrid Undset, the Nobel prize-winner. My grandmother had been sent to town after some Korch, and how my grandfather reacted when she came home has not been recorded. The point is, Erichsen understood that he shaped the physical space around the encounter between reader and book. This encounter can be a delicate one, but he knew how to enter it with dignity. And curiosity, something no book can live without. In short, Erichsen was doing some cultural outreach in his bookshop, and when he died, the next person who managed the shop knew that he too should try to see his patrons as something greater than they sometimes might see themselves. He also understood that he served as literature's outstretched hand, and that if he didn't believe in literature, he wouldn't be able to believe in his customers—or worse, in the intimacy between one consciousness and another. And it is the author who writes literature, and even if she might come across as a pathetic, even laughable figure in person, she's still the horse's mouth. If nothing else, Erichsen respected that. I know, for there was also an old man standing in Erichsen's Bookshop when I was young, and he pulled me over to the shelf with Jorge Luis Borges one day when I was intending to buy something frivolous—the selfsame Borges who wrote:

A book is not an isolated being: it is a relationship,
an axis of innumerable relationships.[*]

In Erichsen's Bookshop, they understood that they were providing the square footage for relationships, whether potential, existing, or broken off. They understood—but do you? That it revolves around intimacy? Perhaps that's what scared me most today: that you did know and then breached it anyway. I won't dare set foot in your shop ever again.

Yours faithfully, etc.

I sent the letter off without hesitating, after which I walked up to the storeroom and dug *Kristin Lavransdatter* out of the box where I'd buried it alive. I didn't want Erichsen to have sold such a thing to a potato farmer's wife in vain.

Translated from the Danish by Misha Hoekstra

[*] "Note on (toward) Bernard Shaw", "Nota sobre (hacia) Bernard Shaw" (1951), translated from the Spanish by James E. Irby, in *Labyrinths*, 1964.

Bohemia Road

IAIN SINCLAIR

The shock of being confronted by the handwritten CLOSING SALE notice hit me like a family bereavement. On Bohemia Road in St Leonards-on-Sea, where fugitive operations peddle war surplus survivalist gear, plastic duck lures, electrified invalid carriages, knitting wool, carnival masks and PVC nurses' outfits, they don't go in for seasonal stock-clearance gimmicks. The stock in Bookmans Halt (no apostrophe, please) is organic: a colony of contented lifers. Armpit tomes mature in the perpetual twilight like mushrooms in a damp cellar. The critical mass of dead paper sustains the integrity of the building. It smells, in the best way, of suspended mortality. This library of ex-library rescues and boot fair probationers is proudly posthumous. The books passed away, honourably, with their previous owners: retirees, hoarding eccentrics and charity cases for whom charity had run out. The stock is buried on the open shelves, to be devoured, piecemeal, by starch-feeding silverfish. Then snorted as legal dust, the cocaine of the underclass, by clinically melancholy customers, silent as Quakers or white-lipped and fugue jabbering like speed freaks. Regulars treat the title above the door—Bookmans Halt—as an order. They freeze on the pavement, check that they are not being followed, before slipping furtively inside to join the permanent wake. The last rites for a significant resource on the point of euthanasia.

My feeling, after visiting Bohemia Road from the time when, having exhausted all other possibilities, I made a desperate punt at dealing, was that the books predated the shop. They were grave goods from some remote Iron Age; tattered remnants of a lost civilization around which the shell of the shop had grown up like an evolving earthwork. Struggling up the steep hill from the station was a pilgrimage, carrying me past the ugly church where a vicar, having fallen into dubious company in the railway pub, conducted conveyor-belt marriages between African gentlemen and Eastern European ladies to whom they had not been previously introduced. My ascent had the same heart-racing anticipation, the same realignment of the body's magnetic poles, as coming down the Ridgeway, after a three-day hike, into the stone circles of Avebury.

Clive Linklater, the proprietor, talked about deciding on a whim to promote the copy of *British Friesian Herd Book Vol. 39* that we'd all come to know and respect. This unlovely item was part of the shop's furniture. And books not only furnished this cave, they propped it up. They buttressed the sagging walls. You felt guilty about lifting even a nicotine-tanned, friable leaflet from one of the mounds of slightly tired arrivals forming stalagmite towers on the floor. When Clive made the *Herd Book* part of his window display, it was the beginning of the end. Double-banked shelves shuddered and creaked. That odd volume was the East Sussex equivalent of the fluttering butterfly wing in China that brings about climate change, tornados in Texas, tsunamis in Thailand. Apocalypse. Finale. Night without end.

Bohemia Road was the perfect address for a functioning used-book pit that represented everything now amputated from the good life in the imaginary state we call England. Here was the antiquarian's equivalent of Orwell's 1946 pub, The Moon Under Water: that muted, gravy-brown boozer existing in no temporal space outside the wet dreams of John Major's speech writers.

Bookmans Halt did exist, on the periphery of reality, for more than fifty years. An authentic address in an authentic suburb of an authentic seaside town. But I could never quite believe it. At first, as a scavenging dealer looking for weekly replenishment for my Camden Passage stall, I parked my car and interrogated the windows of other deluded Bohemia Road enterprises, hoping that Clive would still be there, still in business. I was often accompanied by a bristling skinhead autodidact known as Driffield, a person who claimed to have inspected every last nest of books on this island. And to have duffed up the pretensions of every trembling trader. The first step of Driffield's downfall came when, licking his blue pencil, snorting and barking like a seal at the wit of his own acid put-downs, he began to compose, in block capitals, *Driffs Guide to All the Secondhand & Antiquarian Bookshops in Britain*. The lesson for this conservative anarchist, a man who once failed with a free bookshop in Notting Hill, where customers viewed his stock with extreme suspicion, was to stay under the radar. You can't be a self-promoting invisible. You can't dodge taxes, bills, bailiffs and creditors if you are constantly puffed in the broadsheets and doing a reliable turn in chequerboard plus fours on television. Driffield was a disappearance waiting to happen. Either by his own volition. Or by the hand of one of the increasing number of furies who pursued him with writs and hammers.

In Driff's first, self-published, difficult to navigate guide, brought out in 1984, Bookmans Halt is glossed as: "A med sized stk of low key bks. Very low prices. Very easy to get on with. Trade & Discuss." High praise. Certainly Clive's shop was a "Driff Special": a place where the megaphone-mouthed ruffian could browbeat and bamboozle the owner into letting him walk away with a sack of plunder for next to nothing. But the point that strikes home now is that, before Thatcherism really bit, before the internet swept away Linklater's brand of freelance poverty dodging, the Hastings catchment area could boast of twelve second-hand bookshops. By the time Driff abandoned his

project and vanished into India for seven years, with the
last guide appearing in 1995, we're down to four bookshops
in Hastings and four in St Leonards. And Driffield is the
soapbox orator, a romancer by other means. He devotes
the first forty-six pages of his guide to stand-up routines,
before starting on the Domesday survey of pre-millennial
bookshops still hanging on. The entry for Bookmans Halt
has now expanded into a riff on book dealers who dare to
become authors (a warning the man himself should have
heeded). "You would think that booksellers would be the
last to write bks, surrounded as they are by bestsellers
that are now forgotten… All Mr Linklater worries about
is selling his own autobiography."

When Clive sent me a copy of *Reflections from a
Bookshop Window* in 1994, I picked up the danger signs.
Most book pit proprietors, slumped at their desks, imagine
themselves as writers. Given half a chance, they would
outperform the charlatans whose over-promoted dross
insulates their hideaways. But somehow they never quite
work up the energy to do it. It takes too much out of them
to keep trespassers and potential thieves, otherwise known
as customers and dealers, away from the stock. Their pygmy
kingdoms are book prisons, where they can take a leisurely
revenge on volumes they hate: the ones that refuse to escape.

Linklater, the most genial and humane of his breed,
tolerated some of the sourest time-wasters on the south
coast with good grace; a snivelling procession of libricidal
neurotics whose empty days were plotted around new

methods of demanding impossible rarities they instantly spurn, quibbling over prices so modest they were being pretty much sponsored to take them away. With bed-ruffled hair, unshaven (and proud of it), Clive was a man who looked as if he should be wearing a tattered goalkeeper's jersey over his pyjamas. He admits, in his brisk and entertaining book, that he would prefer to be watching football on the flickering television set he has wedged in a corner than fending off potential purchasers. In fact, he'd prefer to be watching anything: pot-bellied darts from an Essex leisure centre, snowboarding, underwater chess. Or even talking for three hours on the phone with Driffield. Who demands a detailed description of Clive's experience of standing in line, waiting for the doors of a church hall to open on a charity book sale in Crowborough, the only adult among a troop of schoolgirl Brownies in uniform.

The final clearance over, Clive can watch football at his leisure or tinker with a further memoir. He is a free man. And we, his parasites, his penny-pinching regulars, are the bereaved. I made the same move a few years earlier. I sold out and slunk into authorship. There is such a powerful connection between the two trades: the honourable and altruistic profession of providing modestly priced reading matter to a hungry but diminishing demographic and the entitled, despised tribe of scribblers who cough out product. Booksellers dream of the pleasures of staying at home, rising late, finessing their notebook jottings into acclaimed masterpieces, while authors, ground down by the drudgery of hackwork for advances that shrink with every book, once the novelty of the first appearance is over, fantasize about finding that delightful antiquarian bookshop in a quiet village tucked against the South Downs.

Between 1975 and 1995, I was a book dealer, first on a weekly stall, then at book fairs; a book dealer (curator, promoter, archaeologist of the re-forgotten and unloved) who wrote, a little, and published from time to time. From 1979, when my own independent press folded (costs skyrocketing, demand shrinking), to 1987, when Mike Goldmark, a barefoot entrepreneur, ace double-glazing salesman, East Midlands bookseller and future gallerist, took an insane risk in publishing my first novel, *White Chappell, Scarlet Tracings*, I produced nothing. Or so I thought. Until it was pointed out by Jeff Johnson, a canny American bibliographer, that my sixty or so book catalogues, taken together, constituted a special kind of novel. He was right. They were advertisements for myself, mini essays, critiques by selection, diatribes against non-payers and the overvalued literary stars of the moment. These self-published booklets were a revenge of the disenfranchised by way of the list, a form previously exploited for short stories by J.G. Ballard and others. The booklets were illustrated and looked not unlike punkish fanzines for alternative lifestyles or counter-cultural manifestos (with price tags).

Without my experience of bounty hunting across the territory, through frontier trading posts like Bookmans Halt (a dozen a day), I would never have found the dynamic for

White Chappell, Scarlet Tracings. I mean the underlying energy system: the metaphor of the marketplace, where nothing is worth more than you can get for it. Driffield and his fellow scavengers were pressed into service as characters. All I had to do was shave off several layers of eccentricity. The real thing would appear grotesquely overwritten. This was a Masonic world of covert circulation, conspiracy, betrayal, addiction, shotgun suicides. A world governed by arcane rules and strict hierarchies. I could track an item, in one week, everybody taking a cut along the way, from the gutters of Brick Lane and Cheshire Street to the crystal cabinets of Savile Row and Covent Garden. A simple but essentially closed system was undone by the arrival of the internet; suddenly all the information was out there and desired titles were either impossible or available for the price of a postage stamp. At a stroke, a subculture governed by gossip, rumour, superstition and bad juju, was undone. Clive Linklater, wedged behind his heaped desk, hidden by protective bulwarks of as yet unpriced purchases, reported that customers now used his shop to note the particulars of items they would track down, at prices even more modest than his own, on Amazon and AbeBooks.

Street-level dealing in the Eighties was a useful demonstration of Thatcherite economics: the survival of the unfittest, those who started out with inherited fortunes and managed, more by luck than judgement, not to lose them. It was in 1980 that I stepped back from poetry and Clive Linklater took over Bookmans Halt, retaining the given

name and carrying the business forward, with a proper
respect (untouched, unimproved), into a more volatile
period. Shell-shocked freelancers reacted to Thatcher's iron
claw in different ways. Some became electively homeless,
lost on the road. Like Driff, who leapt straight onto one
of Lord Tebbit's mythic bikes, they were rootless in pur-
suit of the deal. The old centre, with its antiquarian book
depositories, was under attack by what Patrick Keiller in
his film *London* saw as a tyranny of the suburbs. You not
only abolish local government, old leftist power bases, but
also *the idea of the local*. You treat locality as a sentimental
indulgence. And you throw the market open to every form
of international money laundering, arms dealing and economic boosterism. An ideal climate for the endgame book
pirate. The one whose only property is a flapping black
attaché case. Whose office is a telephone in a motorway
service station.

Many of those traumatized, chemically fuelled desper-
ados—the ones I called "out-patients"—were remnants of
the dream of the Sixties: almost rock stars, unsponsored
poets, premature ecologists, hedge scholars without tenure.
Writers, attached to the myth of heroic modernism, collected books and texts, to excuse themselves from the
trouble of writing them. Through my catalogues I met a
number of artists, film-makers and archivists who justified
the hoarding of locked-room mysteries, pseudonymous
drug shockers, lesbian vampire porn, leather-boy pulps,
surrealism, uranianism, Ripperology, by seeing this fetish

as a discipline for sustaining cultural value. In the way that Ray Bradbury's characters in *Fahrenheit 451* took on themselves the responsibility of committing books to memory in a period when libraries were condemned to be burnt. And that sense of exile from the political nexus, of random movement, is seductive. Chris Petit's 1979 film, *Radio On*, stretches its time frame to feature length by electing to take the old road from London to Bristol—with a psychotic squaddie from Northern Ireland, Silbury Hill, frozen English fields and pylons, and the nervy soundtrack of the moment. It's a classic book-hunting trip, without books. Petit became one of my steadiest customers, building up a Soho bibliography for his novel *Robinson* as soon as the economics of independent film-making collapsed.

I have demonstrated how the atmosphere of predatory book dealing in the Seventies and Eighties infected my prose style. Those sketches of Bookmans Halt in its last days are, obviously, overcoloured and in love with entropy. But they are no crueller than Linklater's own *Withnail and I* diary of a year's reckless trading gambits. Clive relishes the uncombed hair, the blackened, bacon-wedged teeth of customers and dealers. The station-sleeping uniform of mildewed coat and fingerless gloves. The fat newspapers, marked for charity sales, doubling as overnight insulation. He knows that Bohemia Road is the ultimate sieve for the floating detritus of abandoned collections, unwilled retirement ballast. Bookmans Halt is the last net before the English Channel. Linklater visits every town within a thirty-five-mile radius of Hastings. "In places where on previous trips I left behind bookshops and antique shops, now I find estate agents and building society branches." He is so desperate to bring something home that he spends £15 on a copy of Mrs Beeton's *Book of Household Management*, previously employed as a chopping board for vegetables, and a Florence Nightingale autograph that proves to be kosher. Unfortunately, it didn't come from the "Lady with the Lamp", but a volunteer, with the same name, working part time in the Bexhill Oxfam shop. This signature, Linklater admits, "is only worth something when it's written on a cheque". The fact that it was written in biro might have been a clue.

I never came away from Bookmans Halt with treasure, but I didn't come away empty-handed either. The bargains, the steals that made my week, turned up in Bury St Edmunds, the Channel Islands, Taunton, Rotterdam, Rutland. That pristine, yellow and red first edition of Bram Stoker's *Dracula* being offered for 50p, because "nobody wants hardbacks these days", alongside a newish paperback with a movie tie-in cover at £2. The copy of John Lennon's *In His Own Write* scraped from the floor under the Portobello Road flyover. The one inscribed by all the Beatles, their girlfriends of the moment, and Helen Shapiro. The Turgenev presented by D.H. Lawrence to Jessie Chambers, the "Miriam" of *Sons and Lovers*. The pocket edition Henry James with his holograph corrections. Such items would not have survived ten minutes in

Linklater's shop. Clive's prices were so modest, his stock so comfortably resident that no visit was time wasted. I thought of a phrase by the poet Lee Harwood, perched down the coast in Hove: "besieged decency". That was what Clive really specialized in. That's what was threatened and now lost.

When I stopped dealing and started writing, I used Bookmans Halt like a reference library. I accessed research materials and oddball items I never knew that I needed. A Saturday morning walk up the hill was my form of beach-combing, without a metal detector. I always returned with a bag of finds to smuggle into the flat, purchased for the price of a couple of weekend broadsheets and much better value.

More than all this carnivalesque detail, Bookmans Halt was a fixed point in a shifting world, even though its interior was under constant revision. Towards the end, when the legend—*where do they come from and where do they go?*—no longer had to be supported, Clive presented me with a yellow scrap of paper on which was outlined a history of Bohemia Road assembled by Edward Preston. You witness the shop dissolving through its various disguises, up there on the ridge at the outer limit of the architect James Burton's vision of a Georgian speculation known as St Leonards-on-Sea. Or, as its promoter would have it, Burton's St Leonards.

In the early years of the twentieth century, number 127 Bohemia Road was occupied by the Liberal Club. The Liberals declining, an antique dealer called Mr Martin took a punt, before handing over to Stone Brothers, man-ufacturers of rat traps. (Strange how just the right names attach themselves to this property. I made a number of expeditions to the south coast with the best scout of his generation, the rock guitarist Martin Stone. Martin was the inspiration for one of the characters in *White Chappell, Scarlet Tracings*. On a run to Hastings, we came across a posthumous collection of books from the library of the Vorticist photographer Alvin Langdon Coburn. I still have a copy of E.A. Wallis Budge's *The Liturgy of Funerary Offerings* with Coburn's occult bookplate.)

It wasn't too long before the Stones decided to give up rats and sidestep into antiques. That didn't last, it never does: the definition of an antique shop at the seaside is a necessary staging post in the process of gentrification, leading to an era of dolled-up, empty properties, ironic T-shirts and generic coffee outlets. A stationer called Quinlan (anticipating the name of the grotesque Orson Welles detective in *Touch of Evil*, the one who is told by Marlene Dietrich that his future is "all used up") failed very quickly, handing over the deeds, in 1923, to a speculator in toys and fishing tackle. Next: a base for missionaries. Next: a ladies' outfitter. After which the premises are split between a specialist in wardrobes (autopsy furniture) and the Hastings Radio and Television Company (transmitting to the dead).

At the dawn of the Sixties, the property played its trump card: used books. Mr J. Simmonds abandons wardrobes and chests of drawers for the shelf-fillers thrown in, as house clearance, for the same price. In 1965 he passes the enterprise on to Mr F. Moore, a retired civil servant, who, after deciding on the name Bookmans Halt, hung on until 1978. Within two years, the enterprising young Clive Linklater found his vocation. The business drifts on, after its own fashion, until 2016. The last of its kind. The book stacks offer encouragement to browsers, fanatics, schoolchildren and hard-bitten dealers (such as Driffield and Stone). Linklater should have been given a heritage grant and a preservation order. He didn't really sell books; he rented them for a modest premium. He sorted the shelved items into approximate categories in something close to alphabetical order. He didn't make a show of having a man already in place for anything asked of him. But he made no promises. He looked properly weary, but never in need of an ambulance. The news of the closure of Bookmans Halt will be remembered by faithful customers like the assassination of Kennedy. A dark day for Hastings. The tide washing wrecked libraries ashore now trickled into an infestation of charity shops and hopeless operations run by struck-off accountants and madmen who dread the idea of underpricing the meanest paperback.

For the first week of the closing sale, every item in the shop was on offer at £1 a time: elephant folios, leather-bound odd volumes, fat art books, military memoirs, movie star puffs, slip-cased Folio Society editions, first editions by unfashionable authors glued to the shelves since the day

Clive opened. The second week the price was 50p. Then whatever was left was hauled away by optimists hoping to launch a shop of their own farther down the coast. Relieved of the burden of the eternal cycle of trade—buy, sell, buy, phone, beg, pray, sell—Clive had time to speak about his true passion: following the professional career, club to club, of Gareth Barry. Barry was a local boy from Hollington. He played football with Clive's son. Now he was at Everton. Clive had been in the pub at lunchtime to watch the Toffees beating Chelsea 2–1. The former Manchester City international, in the twilight years of his stellar career, was buying up substantial tranches of property around Bohemia Road as an investment. It would close the circle very neatly if he ended up with Bookmans Halt in his portfolio.

A couple of weeks later, coming west down the Grand Parade, alongside the shell of the burnt-out pier, I met the revived Mr Linklater, strolling with his wife (never previously seen), and pushing a grandson in his buggy. It is often a shocking thing to encounter a bookshop troglodyte in the open air. But Clive was smiling, ruddy, burnished by pale winter sunshine. He was enjoying his new life. I was carrying a pair of fresh-caught plaice and a leaky bottle of fill-on-demand rosé in my bookshop bag. The wine merchant, recently down from London, featured a small collection of books for sale and an exhibition of works by Hastings notables like Aleister Crowley and Robert Tressell. But, after the closure of Bookmans Halt, I was in denial. I didn't have the spirit to poke through lesser stock.

Taking my leave of Clive, I realized that my book bag, the biggest and strongest I owned, bore the stamp of Maggs Bros: "By Appointment to Her Majesty the Queen, Purveyors of Rare Books & Manuscripts". An unnecessarily capacious receptacle, since I'd never bought so much as a pamphlet from the alarming Berkeley Square premises. Clive, when I was carrying off a dozen bargains, offered a thin blue Asian minimart carrier bag. By coincidence, the chill blast of economic realism was being felt, at exactly this moment, by Clive Linklater in Bohemia Road, St Leonards-on-Sea, and Ed Maggs, managing director of the most prestigious antiquarian operation in the land, in Berkeley Square, Mayfair.

At the time when I was first raiding Bookmans Halt to restock my Camden Passage stall, Ed Maggs was starting his apprenticeship in the family firm. He began humping boxes and typing invoices in 1980, the year that Linklater became his own boss. From time to time, Ed appeared at my Islington stall. He was as genial as Clive, with a not dissimilar backstory around music, playing in a band and acting as DJ in subterranean clubs. Founded by Uriah Maggs in 1853, and holding out in Berkeley Square, among the Rolls-Royce showrooms, the intimidating eighteenth-century property where the great antiquarian firm operated was just a fancy version of Bookmans Halt. Maggs Bros bought favoured items at auction for millions rather than snatching them away, as Clive was obliged to do, from the ring of Sussex cowboys for the price of a bottle of rotgut. Both buildings were haunted. The one in Mayfair by some wandering spectre from the days of stables and maidservants. And the one on Bohemia Road by the revenants of a lost life, the vanished bookmen and paper addicts.

As Bookmans Halt gave up the ghost, Maggs Bros startled the trade—it was like Westminster Abbey floating downstream in the night—by relocating to temporary premises, modest in scale, in Curzon Street. The gig was up. It felt as if books, like rat traps and Liberals, were a passing fad. Property, it appears, is an absolute. Occupations flourish and fade. It is the characters, the frustrated rock stars and authors of memoirs, who bring place to life. Who provide jobbing writers with their inspiration. Even if, as Ginsberg says, we have to publish in eternity.

My Homeland
Is Storyland

ELIF SHAFAK

T here is no place like Storyland for lonely children growing up in broken homes. I know, because I was one of them.

I was raised as a single child by a single mother at a time and in a land where this was quite unusual. It all started—from my point of view, that is—in Strasbourg. A small flat crammed with leftist-liberal Turkish students, cigarette smoke, revolutionary ideas, heated political discussions and lots of books. Shortly afterwards my parents went their separate ways. My father stayed in France to complete his doctorate in philosophy. My mother and I came to Turkey. Mum was too young, confused. She had no diploma since she had dropped out of university when she decided to get married. Love would be enough, she had thought. As a result, she now had no job, no money. Moreover, she was a "divorcee"—not a good word in The Advanced Dictionary of Patriarchy.

In this state we arrived in my maternal grandmother's home in Ankara. In my memories this two-storey house changes all the time: sometimes it's the colour of sour cherries; at other times, of salted plums or pickled beetroots. What does not change is the fact that it was located in a very conservative, patriarchal Muslim neighbourhood. Smells of fried aubergine, crushed garlic and scattered rosewater wafted from the open windows. Curious eyes blinked behind every curtain—watching, judging.

To my dismay, there were no bookshops in the vicinity. No libraries within sight. Later on, when we were invited to the neighbours' houses I would notice that there were bookshelves in several of them, but usually these were meant for purposes other than holding books. Most of the cabinets in the "guest rooms" were decorated with porcelain kittens, sets of delicate tea glasses or gilded coffee cups. There were also a number of wedding photographs with absurd backgrounds of wild orchids and flying geese, the likes of which I had never seen before. But very few books.

That doesn't mean, of course, there were no books. Every house had a copy of the Qur'an, for instance. And probably volumes of Hadiths (sayings of Prophet Muhammad) and Islamic prayers. I had realized, as a child, that people preferred to keep the holy book hanging on the wall inside a precious silk cover—untouchable, unreadable, aloof. But weren't books meant to be read? Why was the holy book up there—above my height? beyond my reach? I would also learn, over the years, that I, as a girl, had to be twice as careful when approaching the Qur'an. I would not be able to touch it, for example, when I had my period. I would be regarded as "dirty" on those days.

It wasn't a literary or intellectual environment, to say the least, the one I found myself in as a child. In the meantime, encouraged by Grandma, my mother had gone back to university to finish her degree. For a while, I called my mother *abla*—big sister—and I called Grandma, the woman who took care of me during those years, *anne*—mum. It was a bit confusing for everyone else, but somehow crystal clear to me.

Grandma was not a well-educated woman but she wholeheartedly believed that girls—even more than boys, she said—should get the best education. She was a healer. People with skin diseases, chronic fatigue or depression came to see her. She also cured the love-struck—those who were possessed by either love or madness, which Grandma said amounted to the same thing. Inside the house it was prayers and superstitions; rose thorns, red apples, evil eye beads, amber rosaries. Meanwhile, outside the house, there were bombs, gunshots and demonstrations. People died. People disappeared. In the late 1970s, just before the *coup d'état*, right wing was fighting against left wing, democrats were fighting against nationalists and Islamists, Kurds were taking up arms, and all of them were fighting among themselves. Political violence galloped.

Grandma was an amazing storyteller. She knew all the love stories by heart—Leila and Majnun; Farhad and Shirin;

Kerem and Asli… They were the Romeos and Juliets of the Middle East. Her stories always began in the same way: "Once there was, once there wasn't…" As soon as I heard this line, I knew I was entering a magical land, a topsy-turvy world where time ran in circles, animals danced and talked and preached, babies rocked their fathers' cradles. Such was Grandma's universe, full of myths, good-natured spells and supernatural creatures made of smokeless fire. They were called the djinn. If you could unveil their names, you could rule over them. Otherwise, they were more likely to command you. Life was very precarious.

On the shelf above the TV, there was a thick, brown tome—*The Big Book of Islamic Interpretation of Dreams*. I was fascinated by it. What kind of a publication was this? It felt like a dictionary, but it wasn't. It was structured like an encyclopedia, but it wasn't that either. At times, it read like a short story or a poem, though clearly this was something else. Love is a puzzle. You don't become besotted only with people, but also with printed works or abstract ideas. I certainly had a massive crush on this particular book.

Every dream was open to interpretation. Every interpretation could be reinterpreted depending on the intention and knowledge of the interpreter. The reader was less a passive consumer than an active contributor. The act of reading was not necessarily linear or logical. Unlike the books I had devoured before, this one had no beginning, no end. It was a labyrinth. I could start reading it in the middle, go backwards, skip pages, jump to and fro as though playing hopscotch with words.

At school, in the classroom, to my immense pleasure, I found a little cabinet full of books, most of them by Turkish authors. I finished them all quickly. Then, finding no other titles to borrow, I reread them, this time more slowly. But writing was an agony. By birth, I was left-handed. Our class teacher had made it very clear that this was a genetic mistake that needed to be corrected through discipline and perseverance. Everyone had to hold their pencils in their right hands.

"When you kids go to the toilet, you clean yourselves with your left hands, no? Therefore, the left hand is your dirty hand. Whereas your writing needs to be clean, pure, immaculate."

Seeing how badly I struggled and suffered in silence, the same teacher pulled me aside one day and advised me to send my left hand into "exile". It was the first time I had heard the word. Hence throughout my primary school years, I tried to keep my left hand, my shameful and sinful hand, under the desk, unseen, unwanted—though, of course, it always re-emerged, refusing to be subjugated. I thus learned that the more you repress something, the stronger it comes back. To this day, my two hands still feel utterly uncoordinated and I find it very difficult to write anything longhand.

A few years later, my mother graduated from university and became a diplomat. The two of us moved to Madrid,

Spain. From the irrational, religious and equally claustrophobic and magical neighbourhood in Ankara, I was zoomed into this posh international school attended by the children of diplomats, bureaucrats and expats. Extremely introverted and timid, once again feeling like an outsider, I retreated into myself like a turtle hiding in her shell. Except my shell was made of books.

I began reading in Spanish—*The Life of Lazarillo de Tormes, His Fortunes and Adversities* left a deep impression on my soul. From a sturdy, blond Dutch boy who had the habit of bullying unpopular kids like myself and already had a list of nicknames in store for me, I learned that Turks had chopped off the left hand of Cervantes. Luckily, he was right-handed. Who was this Cervantes, I wondered. The day I discovered *Don Quixote* was a most glorious day: here were an indomitable will to adventure and individuality, a relentless imagination, an unlikely, almost ridiculous hero, and that sad old gap between the real and the possible. It all resonated with me. English, at the time, was the third language in my life but I fell in love with it fast and hard. Charles Dickens, Enid Blyton, Roald Dahl, Oscar Wilde, and then one day, Jane Austen.

In my early twenties I arrived in Istanbul, believing with all my heart that the city was calling me. Tiny serpentine streets with crazy graffiti, layers of history, a beguiling combination of smells and sounds, an urban magnet of collective amnesia and personal stories that were waiting to be told. And bookshops. How I loved them.

My favourite shops were around the Istiklal Avenue close to the Taksim Square. One of them was Simurg, named after the mythical bird that lived in the Tree of Knowledge—the staff were always friendly and kind but they also let you peruse as much as you wanted. Piles of books, little stools to sit on, many of which were occupied by cats of all colours. They would watch the customers, their eyes narrowed down to slits. Another store was Robinson Crusoe, which stocked such a wide range of titles, from travel books to art history, that you could spend hours in here without realizing it. As a curious and somewhat disoriented reader, I would purchase whatever drew my attention, both in English and in Turkish. The classics of British, French, Russian and South American literature; contemporary American, Scandinavian, Italian authors; Sufi and Jewish mystics; Persian and Indian poets; cultural history; German political philosophy; Greek poets and writers—beloved Kavafis and Kazancakis.

Then, once a week, I would hop onto the ferry and cross to the Asian side of the city. In Kadikoy, I had two other cherished bookshops. These were very different from the ones on the European side of the city. They were much more messy, for instance, the aisles cluttered with all kinds of miscellaneous articles, a chaotic jumble. Heavy metal posters, badges of Turkish and European rock bands, handbags with feminist symbols, mugs with leftist poems, notebooks with environmentalist slogans…

From the small, dingy teahouses nearby, you could grab a cup of linden tea or strong coffee, then light a cigarette and keep looking at the books or even finish reading them. Nobody would mind if you smoked inside these bohemian bookshops. Hence the smells of tobacco, coffee and linden mixed with the smells of books. It is a wonder that we didn't burn the place down. The staff—young men, and a few women, who always wore black T-shirts and were often high on weed—couldn't care less what the customers did, so long as they did not steal. Anything and everything that was counter-culture was lumped together in an astonishing mixture and scattered amongst the books on sale. It was pure confusion. And confusion was, and still is, what we Turks do best.

During those years, I not only loved, adored and breathed Istanbul, but also quarrelled with the metropolis endlessly. In my novels, I wrote about its stories, yet just as much about its silences, secrets, taboos and shames. To me the city has always been a strong character in her own right, throbbing with energy, never just a colourful backdrop or mere melancholic scenery. The longer I lived here the more I was convinced that Istanbul was a she-city. Although the streets and the public squares belonged to men, especially after sunset the soul of Constantinopolis was that of a woman refusing to age.

So there I was, for a long time, back and forth on ferries, visiting the bookshops on the opposite shores of the city. I would buy literary classics and academic titles from the shops on the European side, and all my counterculture books, magazines and fanzines from the shops on the Asian side. It could have been the exact opposite, however, since the two shores of the city are not divided along clear-cut cultural lines.

The other places I visited regularly were *sahaflar*—second-hand bookshops. Many of these were not exactly shops, but rather ramshackle huts full of a mesmerizing range of manuscripts and miniatures and magazines, as well as forgotten—sometimes banned—publications. The clientele would be different here, somehow more serious-looking. Elderly readers could be spotted alongside university students. Silence would reign. No smoking, no heavy metal music, definitely no weed. When you opened an old Ottoman book, you could see a prayer on the first page dedicated to Kebikec—the name of the djinni that was supposed to protect books from dust and destruction.

All this time, I kept my reading lists eclectic, a patchwork of different cultures, genres and pasts. There was no order, no hierarchy, no centre. Where did the East start and where did the West end? I drew my own imaginary maps, where stories travelled freely across the boundaries of countries and continents, nations and religions. Without a care whether it was deemed "highbrow" or "lowbrow" literature, I devoured anything that intrigued me, from the Frankfurt School to Ottoman women's magazines.

Over the years, I moved from Istanbul to Boston, Michigan to Arizona, then back to Istanbul again and, eventually, London.

But the bookshops of Istanbul, and their chaos and diversity, keep travelling with me. I carry them everywhere. Inside my head, inside my soul…

WRITERS' BIOGRAPHIES

ALAA AL ASWANY originally trained as a dentist, and still has his own dental practice in Cairo. *The Yacoubian Building* was longlisted for the International IMPAC Dublin Literary Award in 2006, has sold over one million copies worldwide, and was the bestselling novel in the Arab world for over five years. Al Aswany is also the author of *Chicago* (named by *Newsday* as the best translated novel of 2006) and *Friendly Fire*. His work has been translated into more than 30 languages, and published in over 100 countries. He speaks Arabic, English, French and Spanish. Al Aswany has received many awards internationally, including the Bashrahil Award for the Arabic novel, the Kafavis Award from Greece, and the Grinzane Cavour Award from Italy, and was recently named by *The Times* as one of the best 50 authors to have been translated into English over the last 50 years.

STEFANO BENNI is widely considered to be one of Italy's foremost writers. His novels include *Bar Sport*, *Terra!*, *The Cafe Beneath the Sea*, *The Company of The Celestini* and *Timeskipper*. His trademark mix of biting social satire and magic realism has made his books national bestsellers, and they have been translated into over 20 languages. He is also the author of several volumes of essays and poetry and many collections of short stories. He lives in Rome.

MICHAEL DIRDA is a Pulitzer Prize-winning literary journalist and a weekly reviewer for the *Washington Post*. His own books include a memoir, several collections of essays, and the 2012 Edgar Award-winning *On Conan Doyle*. In 2015 he brought out *Browsings: A Year of Reading, Collecting, and Living with Books*. Forthcoming is an appreciation of late 19th and early 20th century popular fiction, tentatively titled *The Great Age of Storytelling*.

HENRY HITCHINGS has written three books about language: *Dr Johnson's Dictionary*, *The Secret Life of Words* and *The Language Wars*. He is also the author of *Who's Afraid of Jane Austen?* and *Sorry! The English and their Manners*. He has won the John Llewellyn Rhys Prize and the Somerset Maugham Award, as well as the Modern Language Association's prize for the best book by an independent scholar. Since 2009 he has been the theatre critic for the *Evening Standard*, and he is consultant editor of the *Oxford English Dictionary*.

DANIEL KEHLMANN is a novelist and playwright, born in Munich. His novels include *Measuring the World*, *Me and Kaminski*, *Fame*, and most recently *F*. He has been awarded the Candide Prize, the Kleist Prize and the Thomas Mann Prize. He lives in Berlin and New York.

ANDREY KURKOV, born in 1961, is a Ukrainian novelist who writes in Russian. He is the author of eighteen novels and seven books for children. His work has been translated into 37 languages, and he has contributed to publications including the *New York Times*, the *Guardian*, *Le Monde*, *Die Welt* and *Die Zeit*. He has also written extensively for the screen. He has been a member of the jury for the Man Booker International Prize, and his own awards include Ukraine's Writer of the Year (2001) and the International Nikolai Gogol Prize (2012). He is currently vice-president of Ukrainian PEN and head of the editorial board of the weekly newspaper *Culture and Life*.

YIYUN LI is the author of two short story collections and two novels, and the winner, most recently, of the *Sunday Times* EFG Short Story Award. A native of Beijing and a graduate of the Iowa Writers' Workshop, she is the recipient of a 2010 MacArthur Foundation fellowship, the Frank O'Connor International Short Story Award, the Hemingway Foundation/PEN Award, the Whiting Writers' Award and the Guardian First Book Award. In 2007 *Granta* named her one of the best American novelists under 35, and in 2010 she was named by the *New Yorker* as one of the twenty most important fiction writers under 40. Her work has appeared in the *New Yorker*, the *Paris Review*, *A Public Space*, *The Best American Short Stories*, and *The O. Henry Prize Stories*. She teaches writing at the University of California, Davis, and lives in Oakland, California.

PANKAJ MISHRA is the author of several books, including *The Romantics: A Novel* and *From the Ruins of Empire: The Revolt against the West and the Remaking of Asia*. He writes political and literary essays for the *Guardian*, the *New Yorker*, the *London Review of Books* and the *New York Review of Books*, and is a columnist for *Bloomberg View* and the *New York Times Book Review*.

DORTHE NORS was born in 1970 in Herning, Denmark and currently lives in Jutland. She holds a degree in literature and art history from the University of Aarhus. In addition to her short story collection *Karate Chop*, she has published two novellas and five novels. Her short stories have appeared in *Harper's Magazine*, *Boston Review*, *AGNI*, *A Public Space*, *Guernica* and the *Guardian*. She is the first Danish writer to have a story published in the *New Yorker*. In 2011, she was awarded the Danish Arts Agency's Three Year Grant for "her unusual and extraordinary talent". In 2014, *Karate Chop* won the P.O. Enquist Literary Prize, and *Publishers Weekly* acclaimed it as one of the best books published in the US in 2014. Her latest book *Mirror, Shoulder, Signal* will be published by Pushkin Press in 2017.

YVONNE ADHIAMBO OWUOR was born in Kenya. She won the 2003 Caine Prize for African Writing and is a past recipient of a Chevening Scholarship and an Iowa Writer's Fellowship. Her story "The Knife Grinder's Tale" was adapted into an award-winning short film. From 2003 to 2005, she was the Executive Director of the Zanzibar International Film Festival. She has also been a TEDx Nairobi speaker and a Lannan Foundation resident. Her debut novel *Dust* was shortlisted for the Folio Prize 2015 and the FT/Oppenheimer Emerging Voices award.

IAN SANSOM is a novelist, journalist and broadcaster. He is the author of the Mobile Library series of novels. His non-fiction includes *The Truth About Babies* and *Paper: An Elegy*. His most recent book is *Westmorland Alone* (2016), novel number 3 in his 44 book series, *The County Guides*.

ELIF SHAFAK is Turkey's most-read woman writer and an award-winning novelist. She is also a public speaker, a political commentator and an activist for women's rights and freedom of speech. She writes in English and in Turkish. Her fourteen books, nine of which are novels, include *The Bastard of Istanbul*, *The Forty Rules of Love*, *Honour*, *The Architect's Apprentice* and the memoir *Black Milk*. Her work, which has been translated into 42 languages, blends Western and Eastern traditions of storytelling. Bringing out the voices of women, minorities, subcultures, immigrants and global souls, it reflects a strong interest in history, philosophy, mysticism, Sufism and gender equality.

IAIN SINCLAIR has lived in (and written about) Hackney, East London, since 1969. His novels include *Downriver* (Winner of the James Tait Black Prize and the Encore Prize for the Year's Best Second Novel), *Radon Daughters*, *Landor's Tower* and *Dining on Stones* (which was short-listed for the Ondaatje prize). Non-fiction books, exploring the myth and matter of London, include *Lights Out for the Territory*, *London Orbital* and *Edge of the Orison*. In the 1990s Sinclair wrote and presented a number of films for BBC2's *Late Show*. He has subsequently co-directed with Chris Petit four documentaries for Channel 4; one of these, *Asylum*, won the short film prize at the Montreal Festival. He edited *London, City of Disappearances*, which was published in 2006. Since then he has published *Hackney, That Rose-Red Empire* (2009), *Ghost Milk* (2011) and *American Smoke* (2013). His account of a one-day walk around the orbital railway—*London Overground*—was published in 2015.

ALI SMITH was born in Inverness in 1962 and lives in Cambridge. Her novels include *Hotel World*, *The Accidental* and *There but for the*. She has been shortlisted for the Booker Prize three times, most recently for *How to be both* (2014), which won the Baileys Women's Prize for Fiction and the Costa Novel Award. She has published five collections of short stories, most recently *Public Library and other stories* in 2015.

SAŠA STANIŠIĆ once hit the bull's-eye when he was shooting, and never again. That was in Višegrad, in former Yugoslavia. There was a sofa in his parents' apartment, with a box beside it where his books were kept, a lot of them all mixed up together. He often lay there among the books, reading. Today he would sometimes like to be that child again—a child whose world consisted of other worlds in which he occasionally fell asleep with his mind at ease.

JUAN GABRIEL VÁSQUEZ was born in Bogotá in 1973. He is the author of a book of stories, *The All Saints' Day Lovers*, and five novels: *The Informers*, *The Secret History of Costaguana*, *The Sound of Things Falling* (winner of the Alfaguara prize in Spain and the IMPAC Dublin Literary Award), *Reputations* (winner of the Premio Real Academia Española and the Prémio Casa de América de Lisboa), and the forthcoming *La forma de las ruinas*. He is the recipient of the Prix Roger Caillois, previously awarded to writers such as Mario Vargas Llosa and Roberto Bolaño. He has translated works by E. M. Forster and Victor Hugo, among others, into Spanish. His books are published in 28 languages worldwide.

ANTHEA BELL, born 1936, daughter of writer Adrian Bell, was educated at Talbot Heath School, Bournemouth and the University of Oxford. She has two sons and twin granddaughters. She has worked for many years as a freelance translator from German and French. Her translations include works of non-fiction; modern literary and popular fiction; books for young people including (originally with co-translator Derek Hockridge) the *Asterix the Gaul* strip cartoon series; and classics by E.T.A. Hoffmann, Freud, Kafka and Stefan Zweig. She has won several translation awards, was appointed OBE in 2010, and was recently awarded the Cross of Merit of the Federal Republic of Germany.

ROSS BENJAMIN is a literary translator living in Nyack, New York. He received a 2015 Guggenheim Fellowship for his work on Franz Kafka's *Diaries*, to be published by Liveright/Norton. His previous translations include Friedrich Hölderlin's *Hyperion*, Kevin Vennemann's *Close to Jedenew*, Joseph Roth's *Job*, Thomas Pletzinger's *Funeral for a Dog*, and Clemens J. Setz's *Indigo*. He was awarded the 2010 Helen and Kurt Wolff Translator's Prize for his rendering of Michael Maar's *Speak, Nabokov* and a 2012 National Endowment for the Arts Fellowship. He was a 2003–2004 Fulbright Scholar in Berlin.

HOWARD CURTIS was born in London, and has translated more than a hundred books from French, Italian and Spanish. He now lives in Norwich, where his favourite bookshop is the wonderful Book Hive.

AMANDA LOVE DARRAGH has spent most of her working life buying, selling, translating and editing books, journals and other texts in Moscow, London and Devon. A librarian at heart, she loves sharing books with her three children (though wishes they would put them back in the right place) and has an apparently incurable cookbook addiction. Amanda won the Rossica Translation Prize in 2009. She has been translating the work of Andrey Kurkov since 2010.

RUSSELL HARRIS, translator, curator, author and editor read Oriental Studies at Balliol College, Oxford. He has contributed to various international reference publications and written books on photographic portraits of

India's ruling princes, early automobiles, the social milieu of ladies' fans in early photographic portraiture, inter alia, and has curated photographic exhibitions throughout Europe and the Middle East. He has translated literary and political works from French and Arabic including Alaa Al Aswany's novel *The Automobile Club of Egypt*, and co-translated Al Aswany's political columns in *Democracy is the Answer*. He currently works as an editor at the Institute of Ismaili Studies, London. When not translating or editing, his secret vice is taking his favourite books to Cairo to have them leather-bound for a song.

MISHA HOEKSTRA has taught creative writing and literature at Brown University and Deep Springs College. He moved to Denmark twenty years ago, where he now writes and performs songs under the name Minka Hoist.

ANNE MCLEAN studied history in London, Ontario and literary translation in London, England. Between those two degrees – before running away to Central America, where she started to learn Spanish – she spent two and a half years working at the Yonge Street branch of Toronto's Book City. These days her favourite *librerías* include the London Review Bookshop and Palinuro in Medellín, Colombia.

PUSHKIN PRESS

Pushkin Press was founded in 1997, and publishes novels, essays, memoirs, children's books—everything from timeless classics to the urgent and contemporary.

Our books represent exciting, high-quality writing from around the world: we publish some of the twentieth century's most widely acclaimed, brilliant authors such as Stefan Zweig, Marcel Aymé, Teffi, Antal Szerb, Gaito Gazdanov and Yasushi Inoue, as well as compelling and award-winning contemporary writers, including Andrés Neuman, Edith Pearlman, Eka Kurniawan and Ayelet Gundar-Goshen.

Pushkin Press publishes the world's best stories, to be read and read again. Here are just some of the titles from our long and varied list. To discover more, visit www.pushkinpress.com.

━━━

THE SPECTRE OF ALEXANDER WOLF
GAITO GAZDANOV
'A mesmerising work of literature' Antony Beevor

SUMMER BEFORE THE DARK
VOLKER WEIDERMANN
'For such a slim book to convey with such poignancy the extinction of a generation of "Great Europeans" is a triumph' *Sunday Telegraph*

MESSAGES FROM A LOST WORLD
STEFAN ZWEIG
'At a time of monetary crisis and political disorder... Zweig's celebration of the brotherhood of peoples reminds us that there is another way' *The Nation*

BINOCULAR VISION
EDITH PEARLMAN
'A genius of the short story' Mark Lawson, *Guardian*

IN THE BEGINNING WAS THE SEA
TOMÁS GONZÁLEZ

'Smoothly intriguing narrative, with its touches of sinister, Patricia Highsmith-like menace' *Irish Times*

BEWARE OF PITY
STEFAN ZWEIG

'Zweig's fictional masterpiece' *Guardian*

THE ENCOUNTER
PETRU POPESCU

'A book that suggests new ways of looking at the world and our place within it' *Sunday Telegraph*

WAKE UP, SIR!
JONATHAN AMES

'The novel is extremely funny but it is also sad and poignant, and almost incredibly clever' *Guardian*

THE WORLD OF YESTERDAY
STEFAN ZWEIG

'*The World of Yesterday* is one of the greatest memoirs of the twentieth century, as perfect in its evocation of the world Zweig loved, as it is in its portrayal of how that world was destroyed' David Hare

WAKING LIONS
AYELET GUNDAR-GOSHEN

'A literary thriller that is used as a vehicle to explore big moral issues. I loved everything about it' *Daily Mail*

BONITA AVENUE
PETER BUWALDA

'One wild ride: a swirling helix of a family saga... a new writer as toe-curling as early Roth, as roomy as Franzen and as caustic as Houellebecq' *Sunday Telegraph*

JOURNEY BY MOONLIGHT
ANTAL SZERB

'Just divine... makes you imagine the author has had private access to your own soul' Nicholas Lezard, *Guardian*